MW01115019

Finding Birds

in

San Diego County, California

by

Henry Detwiler

This book is dedicated to my wife Suzanne, who has encouraged me to research and write this guide since I put together the Yuma bird-finding book, and has supported me in every way possible.

© 2016, Henry Detwiler

All rights reserved
ISBN 978-1-329-94700-9
April 2016, Version 1

Front Cover Photograph: White-tailed Kite
Back Cover Photograph: Spotted Towhee

All photos and illustrations by Henry Detwiler

Finding Birds in San Diego County, California

Table of Contents

Introduction to Birding in San Diego County

Why San Diego County?

San Diego County has many wonderful and varied habitats. From the sparkling cold Pacific Ocean to the Laguna Mountains to the shimmering hot Anza Borrego Desert, this county offers birders an unparalleled experience. Millions of birds follow the Pacific Flyway as they migrate north and south along the western coast. The county bird list reflects this variety, too, with a remarkable tally of over 500 species, the highest in the United States.

There's something for everyone here, whether you like plying the high seas for pelagics, kicking up the sand as you search for shorebirds, listening to the sounds of the marsh denizens, trekking after elusive quail in the forests, strolls in urban parks, or enjoying a spectacular bloom of desert flowers as you search for sparrows and thrashers.

If you like "Big Days" this is the county for you. Over 150 species is a reasonable goal in any season, and if you have a good push of migrants and are willing to put some miles on your vehicle, you'll be shooting for 200.

The weather is also remarkable here, with an average temperature of 72 degrees Fahrenheit and just 6" of annual rainfall. Winter brings the most moisture and there may be fog along the coast, but more often than not it clears up before the morning is over.

Seasonal Birding Calendar

- **January** – Look for raptors and first breeders
  - Falcons and accipiters hunt in urban and agricultural areas.
  - Anna's, Allen's, and Costa's Hummingbirds perform display flights and Western Screech-Owls and Great Horned Owls call to each other in preparation for breeding.
- **February** – Thrashers are singing and breeding
  - This is the best month to find Le Conte's and Crissal Thrashers in Anza Borrego State Park.
  - The first Cliff Swallows return and Violet-green Swallows start passing through.
- **March** – A fine combination of wintering and migrating birds
  - Waterfowl and raptors head north out of the area.

- o Spring migrants like Black-chinned Hummingbird, Warbling Vireo, Lucy's Warbler, and Hooded and Bullock's Orioles begin to arrive from the south.
- **April** – Peak of migrant and breeding activity
  - o Migration usually peaks during the last week of April. Good places to check for flycatchers, vireos, and warblers are Point Loma and the numerous city and county parks.
  - o Check desert areas like Tamarisk Grove Campground for singing and calling Verdin, Black-tailed Gnatcatchers, Cactus Wren, Phainopepla, Scott's Oriole, and Lawrence's Goldfinch.
- **May** – Migration still going strong
  - o Continue to check urban parks, green neighborhoods, and riparian zones for warblers and flycatchers.
- **June** – Look for eastern vagrants among the breeding birds
  - o Early in the month keep an eye out for eastern vagrants (Baltimore Oriole, Northern Parula, and American Redstart are just a few to watch out for) which show up along riparian corridors and in urban green zones.
- **July** and early **August** – Shorebirds and hummingbirds come south
  - o Look through the large shorebird flocks at the San Diego River estuary next to Robb Field.
  - o Check flowers and feeders around San Diego and in the mountains for Anna's, Rufous, Allen's, and Black-chinned Hummingbirds.
  - o First passerine migrants also start heading south.
- Late **August** and **September** – Fall migration
  - o Look for passerines in riparian areas along the Tijuana River and San Diego parks.
  - o Shorebirds are still streaming through in good numbers; check for rarities like Curlew Sandpiper and Ruff.
  - o The first migrant/wintering ducks and geese return to the area.
- **October** – Look for vagrants and returning winter residents
  - o Keep checking the shorebirds. This is a good time to spot a vagrant Ruff and look for the rare (but regular) Pacific Golden-Plover.
  - o Red-breasted Sapsucker, Fox Sparrow, rare Clay-colored Sparrow, and other wintering birds return.
  - o Search for eastern vagrant warblers like American Redstart, Black-throated Green Warbler, and Northern Parula in riparian and urban green zones.

- o During some years Red-throated Pipit can be found at the Tijuana River Valley sod farm or other grassy areas like Fiesta Island.
- o Look for western and (rare but regular) eastern orioles: Hooded, Bullock's, Baltimore, and Orchard.
- **November**
  - o Most wintering loons, grebes, Brant, and other waterfowl have returned.
  - o Wintering raptors are back; look for Ferruginous Hawk and Prairie Falcon in the Ramona Grasslands Preserve west of Ramona.
  - o Wintering sparrows are back; look for Golden-crowned Sparrows at Point Loma and elsewhere in coastal brush
- **December** – another opportunity to search for rare northern visitors
  - o Check for rare gulls along the coast.
  - o Look for unusual or rare waterfowl like Long-tailed Duck, Harlequin Duck, Black and White-winged Scoters, and Barrow's Goldeneye.
  - o Check Fiesta Island and other large grassy patches for wintering longspurs.

Target Birding in San Diego County

Visitors to a new area often wish to know where and when they can find a particular species. For example, where can I find that Tricolored Blackbird or the California Gnatcatcher, and when is the best time to look for them?

The chart below recommends likely locations and seasons to find some of the more sought-after California target species. These are by no means the only spots you can find the indicated species, just some of the better-known areas. These birds are in American Ornithological Union (A.O.U.) 7th Edition order, 56th supplement, from July 2015.

Status codes are often a mystery, and depend on all sorts of variables, such as weather, birder's experience level, time of day, and the number of pets or people in the area. Nonetheless, they do give you some idea on how likely you are to see a particular bird if everything goes well. The codes I use are:

C – Common, usually found 3 out of every 4 visits
U – Uncommon, usually located only 1 out of every 4 visits
R – Rare, usually not seen, and may be absent some years

V – Vagrant, does not regularly occur here; often a lost "visitor" from Mexico or the eastern United States—but still, keep an eye out for it!

SPECIES	GOOD LOCATION(S)	SEASON	STATUS
Wood Duck	Lindo Lake County Park	all year	C
All scoter species	Imperial Beach Pier	winter	R-C
Mountain Quail	- Laguna Recreation Area - Kitchen Creek Road	spring	U
California Quail	Jacumba	summer	C
Red-throated Loon	Quivira Basin	winter	U
Black-vented Shearwater	La Jolla Cove	winter	C
Brandt's Cormorant	- La Jolla Cove - Sunset Cliffs	all year	C
Pelagic Cormorant	Point Loma	winter	U
Little Blue Heron	San Diego River Estuary	all year	C
Reddish Egret	Imperial Beach Salt Works	all year	U
Yellow-crowned Night Heron	Imperial Beach Sports Complex	spring	C
Red-shouldered Hawk	- Foothills - Laguna Mountains	all year	C
Ferruginous Hawk	Ramona Grasslands Preserve	winter	U
Ridgway's Rail	- Tijuana Slough NWR - San Elijo Lagoon	spring	C
Black Oystercatcher	Cabrillo National Monument	winter	R
Pacific Golden-Plover	Tijuana Slough NWR	winter	R
Snowy Plover	- Tijuana Slough NWR (breeding) - San Diego River Estuary	summer winter	U
Wandering Tattler	- La Jolla Cove - Sunset Cliffs	winter	C
Black Turnstone	- Cabrillo Nat. Monument - La Jolla Cove	winter	C
Red Knot	San Diego River Estuary	winter	U
Surfbird	- La Jolla Cove - Sunset Cliffs	winter	C
Heermann's Gull	- La Jolla Cove - Sunset Cliffs	all year	C
Western Gull	- La Jolla Cove - Sunset Cliffs	all year	C
Glaucous-winged Gull	- San Diego River Estuary - Chula Vista Bayfront Park	winter	C

SPECIES	GOOD LOCATION(S)	SEASON	STATUS
Least Tern	San Diego Bay	summer	C
Royal Tern	San Diego River Estuary	winter	U
Elegant Tern	San Diego River Estuary	summer	C
Black Skimmer	San Diego River Estuary	summer	C
Burrowing Owl	San Diego River Estuary	all year	U
Spotted Owl	William Heise County Park	spring	U
Northern Saw-whet Owl	Laguna Mountains	spring	R
Vaux's Swift	San Elijo Lagoon	spring	U
Anna's Hummingbird	San Elijo Lagoon	all year	C
Costa's Hummingbird	Anza Borrego State Park	early spring	U
Rufous Hummingbird	San Elijo Lagoon	late summer	U
Allen's Hummingbird	San Elijo Lagoon	all year	U
Acorn Woodpecker	Laguna Recreation Area	all year	C
Red-breasted Sapsucker	- Lindo Lake County Park - Cuyamaca Rancho State Park	winter	U
Ladder-backed Woodpecker	Anza Borrego State Park	spring	U
Nuttall's Woodpecker	- Cuyamaca Rancho State Park - San Elijo Lagoon	all year	C
White-headed Woodpecker	- Cuyamaca Rancho State Park - Palomar Mountain	all year	R
Peregrine Falcon	San Elijo Lagoon	winter	U
Olive-sided Flycatcher	Laguna Mountains	spring	U
Cassin's Kingbird	- Tecolote Canyon Natural Park - Robb Field	winter	U
Bell's Vireo	Tijuana Valley	spring	C
Gray Vireo	Buckman Springs	spring	U
Cassin's Vireo	Palomar Mountain State Park	spring	U
Violet-green Swallow	Laguna Mountains	summer	C
Oak Titmouse	Laguna Mountains	all year	C
Pygmy Nuthatch	Laguna Mountains	all year	C
Canyon Wren	Buckman Springs	spring (singing)	U
Cactus Wren	Anza Borrego State Park	all year	C
California Gnatcatcher	San Elijo Lagoon	spring	C

9

SPECIES	GOOD LOCATION(S)	SEASON	STATUS
Wrentit	Cabrillo National Monument	all year	C
Western Bluebird	Laguna Recreation Area	winter	U
California Thrasher	Jacumba	all year	C
Le Conte's Thrasher	Anza Borrego	spring	R
Phainopepla	Jacumba	spring	C
Longspurs	Mission Bay Park, Fiesta Island	winter	V
Grace's Warbler	Point Loma	winter	V
Northern Waterthrush	Dairy Mart Ponds	winter	V
Painted Redstart	Point Loma	winter	V
Rufous-crowned Sparrow	- Mission Trails Regional Park - Kitchen Creek Road	spring	U
California Towhee	Point Loma	all year	C
Black-chinned Sparrow	Cibbets Flat Campground	spring	C
Black-throated Sparrow	Anza Borrego State Park	spring	C
Nelson's Sparrow	Tijuana Estuary	winter	V
Golden-crowned Sparrow	Point Loma	winter	C
Blue Grosbeak	Dairy Mart Ponds	summer	C
Tricolored Blackbird	Jacumba Pond	spring	C
Scott's Oriole	- Anza Borrego State Park - Jacumba	spring	U
Lawrence's Goldfinch	Kitchen Creek Road	summer	U
Scaly-breasted Munia	Tecolote Natural Canyon Park	summer	C

Birding in the Desert

Be prepared. Parts of Anza Borrego State Park are remote desert areas without drinking water—take along plenty of water (2 gallons of water per person per day is recommended by many experts). Let someone know your schedule, and realize that there is no cell phone coverage in some of these remote areas. Take a good map with you—the line drawings in this book do not show all roads and may not be exactly to scale. Take the appropriate type of vehicle, and be aware that road conditions can change overnight during heavy rains. If you break down, the best advice is to wait by your vehicle for help.

Summer birding in the desert is best avoided, when daily temperatures often soar above 100° and the birds seem to have disappeared in the shimmering heat waves. Winter is often beautiful, but always be prepared for cold weather—even snow in the higher portions of San Diego County. Spring is usually beautiful, but even then it can be hot, rainy, or cold. February and March are great for spring wildflowers after a wet winter. April is usually the best time for birding in the desert, with residents breeding and migrants moving through the washes.

Watch out for bushes, trees, and cacti with thorns. Carrying a multi-tool with pliers is wise; it's a good way to remove cactus spines from boots, pant legs, and tender skin.

Birding on Private Land

Many of the sites listed in this book adjoin private property. Please do not enter these areas without first asking permission from the property owner.

Birding References

One of the best reference books for San Diego County breeding birds is the *San Diego County Bird Atlas*, by Philip Unitt, 2004, San Diego Natural History Museum.

The San Diego Field Ornithologists meet monthly and promote birding in San Diego County: http://www.sandiegofieldornithologists.org/.
The site to check for recent sightings is:
https://groups.yahoo.com/neo/groups/SanDiegoRegionBirding/info.
You can also find the same information at: http://birding.aba.org/, which serves as a clearing house for world-wide rare and unusual bird reports.

Mary Beth Stowe has put together an expansive website with driving routes and hiking trails through her favorite birding locations in San Diego County. The descriptions are accompanied by bird frequency charts compiled from 2003-2008 and a wealth of scenic photos. It's a great resource located at
http://www.miriameaglemon.com/Birding%20Pages/San%20Diego%20Birding%20Pages/By%20Site/San%20Diego%20Site%20Index.html

Short descriptions and a map showing the locations of nine South San Diego County parks is available at
http://www.sandiegocounty.gov/content/dam/sdc/parks/BrochuresMiscellaneous/South_County_Parks_English_Brochure.pdf

Our website at http://www.southwestbirders.com/ has trip reports for many of these birding locales and will have updates to the sites listed in this book. If you have suggestions or comments about this guide, please send them to Henry Detwiler at: *henrydetwiler@earthlink.net*

Chapter Layout

The chapters are organized by areas radiating out from the city of San Diego, which is the first chapter. The coastal zone is next, and covers important areas like the Tijuana River Valley, La Jolla, and San Elijo Lagoon. Palomar Mountain is next. Following that are sites in southern San Diego County, chiefly the Laguna Mountains. Anza Borrego State Park and the desert communities are the final section.

Each chapter is organized in the same way, with descriptions of the most common habitats, target birds you might wish to search for, a general description of the area, one or more maps of the area with numbers and letters that pinpoint birding locations, descriptions of the birding locations themselves, driving directions, and specific site notes for the area.

Under the **Target Birds** heading will be birds that you are likely to find at this location, depending on the season you visit. *Resident* means the bird is likely to be found at the location year-round, and probably breeds there. *Migration* means the bird is found there during either the northern migration in March, April, or May, or during the southern migration in August, September, or October. *Winter* means the bird winters in the area during the months of November-February.

Under the **Driving Directions** I've tried to be as specific as possible, and get you to the birding location in the most direct fashion. However, take a map and/or GPS and understand that some of the back roads are prone to washouts in storms.

Under the **Site Notes** I've identified specific locations where gas, food, and other services may be available. Please don't take these as endorsements of fine food or excellent service—they are merely mentioned here as a convenience. The information is current as of 2015.

This book focuses on 19 general birding areas, which are only a portion of the good spots in San Diego County. Some of the other very nice birding locations are summarized in the final chapter on miscellaneous birding sites. In future versions of this guide I plan to expand on several of these sites with maps and make them full chapters.

Special thanks to Bob Miller for his contributions in the chapter on the Anza-Borrego Desert.

San Diego County Map and Birding Locations

This basic map of San Diego County shows the relative locations of the birding sites described in this book. The letters match the chapter and site names, and are listed in the Table of Contents. More detailed maps and driving directions to each of these sites are contained within the chapters themselves.

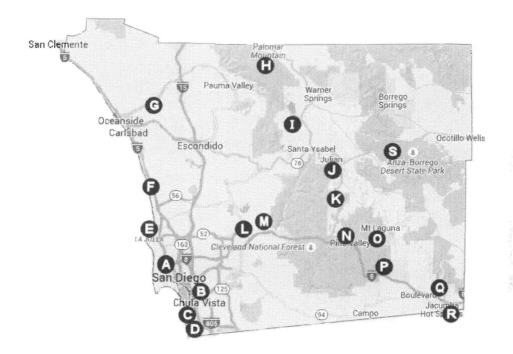

A. **San Diego**
    o   Point Loma
    o   Cabrillo National Monument
    o   San Diego Bay
    o   San Diego Estuary
    o   Mission Beach – Quivira Basin
    o   Sunset Cliffs
    o   Balboa Park
    o   Tecolote Canyon
B. **Chula Vista Bayfront Park (J Street Mudflats)**
C. **Imperial Beach**
    o   Tijuana River National Estuarine Research Reserve
    o   Tijuana River Mouth
    o   Imperial Beach Pier
    o   Imperial Beach Sports Park
    o   South Bay Salt Works
D. **Tijuana River Valley**
    o   Bird and Butterfly Garden

13

- Dairy Mart Ponds
- Sod Farm

E. La Jolla

F. San Elijo Lagoon
   - N. Rios Avenue Trails
   - Visitor Center and Trails

G. Guajome Regional Park

H. Palomar Mountain State Park

I. Lake Henshaw and Mesa Grande Road

J. Julian Area
   - Banner Grade
   - William Heise County Park
   - The Birdwatcher

K. Cuyamaca Rancho State Park
   - Green Valley
   - Paso Picacho Campground
   - Visitor Center and Museum
   - Stonewall Mine
   - Lake Cuyamaca

L. Mission Trails Regional Park

M. Lindo Lake County Park

N. Pine Valley

O. Laguna Recreation Area
   - Sunrise Highway
   - Wooded Hill Trail
   - Agua Dulce Spring
   - Burnt Rancheria Campground
   - Visitor Center
   - Desert View Picnic Area
   - Laguna Campground

P. Buckman Springs Area
   - Sheephead Mountain Road
   - Boulder Oaks Campground
   - Lake Morena County Park

Q. Kitchen Creek Road
   - Cameron Truck Trail
   - Yellow Rose Spring
   - Cibbets Flat Campground

R. Jacumba Hot Springs

S. Anza Borrego Desert State Park
   - Barrel Springs
   - Old Mine Road
   - Culp Valley
   - Borrego Valley
   - Tamarisk Grove Campground
   - Vallecito Stage Station County Park
   - Agua Caliente County Park

A. San Diego Area

Habitat
- Ocean and seashore
- Lakes
- Marshes
- Riparian
- Chaparral
- Urban neighborhoods
- Parks

Target Birds
- Brant (winter)
- Scoters (winter)
- Loons: Red-throated and Pacific (winter)
- Grebes: Horned and Eared (winter)
- Brandt's Cormorant (resident)
- Little Blue Heron (resident)
- Ridgway's Rail (resident)
- Black Oystercatcher (winter)
- Pacific Golden-Plover (rare, winter)
- Snowy Plover (resident)
- Red Knot (winter)
- Gulls: Western and Heermann's (resident), Bonaparte's and Mew (migration and winter)
- Terns: Least (summer), Royal (winter), and Elegant (summer)
- Black Skimmer (summer)
- Great Horned Owl (resident)
- Burrowing Owl (resident)
- Nuttall's Woodpecker (resident)
- Peregrine Falcon (winter)
- California Gnatcatcher (resident)
- Wrentit (resident)
- California Thrasher (resident)
- Western warblers (migrants) and eastern warblers (vagrants)
- California Towhee (resident)
- Golden-crowned Sparrow (winter)
- Scaly-breasted Munia (resident)

General Description

San Diego's praises have been sung in many quarters, and with good reason. It has an ideal year-round climate, a great variety of natural areas, beautiful scenery, and an abundance of birds. And if your significant other isn't a birder, San Diego offers excellent cultural attractions, lots of amusement parks and beaches, and unexcelled shopping opportunities.

No matter the season, there are always birds around. In particular, winter is an excellent time to visit, especially if you're coming from the cold north. Every year local experts track down and monitor the locations of wintering oddities and vagrants like Thick-billed Kingbird, Hepatic and Summer Tanagers, Grace's and Black-throated Green Warblers, and Baltimore and Orchard Orioles.

There are numerous parks and neighborhoods with trees, lawns, and open spaces. The ocean and shoreline offer countless viewing locations for waders, shorebirds, waterfowl, and even some pelagics. Areas of coastal chaparral are home to unique birds like California Gnatcatcher, California Thrasher, and Wrentit. San Diego covers a lot of territory, and new bird-rich spots are continually being discovered. Included in this chapter are some of the better-known locales that have yielded specialties, vagrants, and other good birds over the years.

Elegant Terns

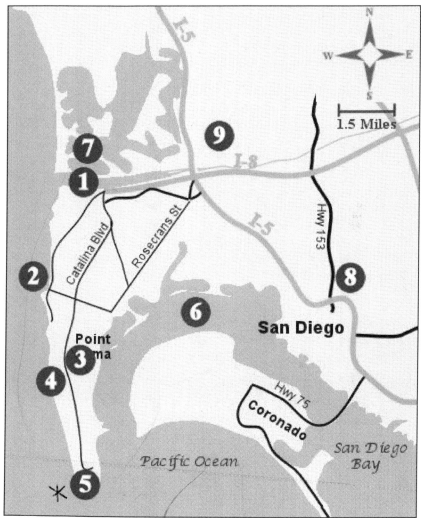

San Diego

Birding Suggestions

1) San Diego River Estuary and Robb Field

This is one of the best and most accessible birding locations in Southern California, located within the community of Ocean Beach. Each season will yield different offerings, but migration and winter have the most variety. There are two unique habitats.

Robb Field: The park, with its large trees and bushes, is a good place to look for breeding Osprey, Cassin's Kingbird, crows, towhees, blackbirds, and orioles. There are usually large crowds here on weekends, so early mornings are best for birding.

San Diego River and Estuary: Visiting this estuary at varying tides will produce differing types of species. During the fall and winter months, high tide will give you a chance for Brant, Horned Grebe, and a fine selection of waterfowl. Lower tides will produce Red Knot, Black-bellied Plover, Snowy Plover, Whimbrel, and Long-billed Curlew. Almost any U.S. shorebird is possible here! Year-round, Little Blue Herons hunt with Snowy and Great Egrets. At times Reddish Egret shows up here. Terns are represented by Least (summer), Black (migration), Common (migration), Forster's (migration), Caspian (resident), Royal (winter), and Elegant (summer). The resident Western Gulls are joined by Herring and rarer gulls during migration and winter. In the fall and winter you'll usually find Mew, Bonaparte's, or Glaucous-winged Gulls. Other frequent visitors are American Skimmer, Double-crested Cormorant, and Savannah Sparrow. It is also possible to access the San Diego River channel from the road to Quivira Basin and the road to Sea World. From these areas you may get better views of resident Ridgway's (Clapper) Rail, Burrowing Owl, and many of the same birds described above.

2) Point Loma – Sunset Cliffs

The community of Sunset Cliffs lies on the west side of Point Loma, just south of Ocean Beach. High sandstone cliffs border the Pacific Ocean, and provide perches for Brown Pelican, Heermann's Gull, and Brandt's Cormorant. You can find the Brandt's

Black Turnstone

Cormorants breeding on a sandstone chimney across from (west of) Froude Street. Especially at low tide, when more of the rocky shoreline is exposed, search in winter for Wandering Tattler, Black Turnstone, and Surfbird.

3) Point Loma – Residential Neighborhoods

The dense trees in some areas (such as Silvergate Avenue) attract a fine array of wintering warblers, including annual rarities like Grace's and Black-throated Green Warblers, Painted Redstart, and various flycatchers.

4) Point Loma – Nazarene University

This beautiful campus has many trees and flowering plants in a park-like setting, combined with some coastal chaparral. Mitred Parakeet and Lilac-crowned Parrot are frequent visitors. Check the numerous flowers for Anna's, Rufous, and Allen's Hummingbirds, especially during their migration in late summer. Warblers and sparrows join the resident birds during migration and winter. During the semester when students are present, your best course of action may be to find an empty parking spot, snag it, and walk around the campus.

5) Point Loma – Cabrillo National Monument

There are two areas of this park to visit: chaparral and tide pools. Park in the main lot close to the visitor center and take one of the numerous trails to explore the large areas of coastal chaparral. California Towhees will often greet you as you exit your vehicle. On the trail you have good opportunities to see California Thrasher, California Quail, and Wrentit. In migration the local birds are joined by western warblers, flycatchers, and sparrows.

Birds of the Coastal Chaparral

California Quail – common resident, but may be difficult to see in the brushy chaparral

Wrentit –common resident, more often heard than seen

California Thrasher – common resident, this bird is often spotted singing from a perch in the spring or summer

California Gnatcatcher – a retiring bird of cactus-studded chaparral

Blue-gray Gnatcatcher – common wintering visitor

Western Scrub-Jay – common and noisy resident; usually responds well to squeaking and pishing

California Towhee – common to abundant resident, but may be hard to spot in the brush; chaparral with lots of open areas like Cabrillo National Monument make seeing them a breeze

Spotted Towhee – common resident; they call often, and will usually perch up if you're patient

Fox Sparrow – common migrant, uncommon winter visitor

The tide pools are very popular on weekends, especially at low tide, when parking may be difficult. During migration and winter look for the typical rock-loving shorebirds, the most common of which is the

Black Turnstone. Also present are Surfbird, Wandering Tattler, and Black Oystercatcher. Rarely, an American Oystercatcher will join the mix. Offshore are the typical terns, gulls, cormorants, and pelicans. Also be on the lookout for Peregrine Falcon, which hunts around the coastal cliffs.

6) San Diego Bay

Least Tern

There are many access points to look out over San Diego Bay, including Shelter Island, Harbor Island, and Silver Strand Blvd. (Highway 75) southeast of Coronado. In the summer look for Least and Elegant Terns, in the winter look for scoters, Brant, grebes, ducks, and gulls. Where there are sections of accessible shoreline (there are several very good pull-offs along Silver Strand) you'll be treated to a wealth of shorebirds, including Red Knot, curlews, turnstones, and numerous sandpipers.

7) Mission Beach – Quivira Basin

During the winter season Quivira Basin is one of the most reliable spots for both Common and Red-throated Loons. Also look for grebes, scoters, and other waterfowl. Gulls and terns may be flying about, and occasionally the rocky embankment for the basin will have a shorebird or two. To the east, on the opposite side of the parking lot, scan the harbor and the piers. Sea lions, cormorants, Brown Pelicans, Great Blue Herons, and egrets all line up at the main boat dock waiting for handouts from the returning fishing boats. It's a fairly reliable spot to see Black-crowned Night Heron, especially early or late in the day.

8) Balboa Park

This 1400-acre urban park has 65 miles of trails, natural zones, open spaces, and gardens. The San Diego Zoo is contained within this park, and attracts many interesting vagrants. Breeding birds at Balboa include Anna's Hummingbird, Nuttall's Woodpecker, Black Phoebe, Cassin's Kingbird, California Towhee, and Hooded Oriole. Winter visitors include waterfowl, Townsend's and Black-throated Gray Warblers, White-crowned and other sparrows, vagrant eastern tanagers, and vagrant eastern orioles. Migrants can include just about

20

any western flycatcher and warbler, as well as regular eastern vagrants. This park can get pretty crowded and noisy, so early in the day is the most productive and enjoyable for birding.

9) Tecolote Canyon Natural Park

This small park has 6.5 miles of trails, recreational facilities, and a new visitor center. The park was named for the Great Horned Owl that calls the canyon home. The trails take you through chaparral habitat which is good for noisy Western Scrub-Jay, retiring Wrentit, California Gnatcatcher (farther up the canyon), surprisingly common California Thrasher, both California and Spotted Towhees, and the omnipresent Bushtit. Allen's Hummingbirds seem to have recently colonized the park (or the neighborhood just to the north). Look for Red-shouldered Hawk, Nuttall's Woodpecker, and Lesser Goldfinch in the park trees. In winter keep an eye open for Merlin, Cooper's Hawk, as well as Cedar Waxwing and wintering warblers. During some years Purple Finch is also present. This is one of several parks in the county which have a resident population of Scaly-breasted Munia. They are often seen in the grass and shrubbery along the canal that borders the north side of the park close to the entrance; they're also not shy about visiting the feeders that several homeowners have set up in their back yards bordering the canal.

Scaly-breasted Munia

Driving Directions to San Diego Locations

- **Area 1 (San Diego River Estuary/Robb Field)** – Follow I-8 west to its terminus, the "T" junction at Sunset Cliffs Blvd. Turn left on Sunset Cliffs Blvd. and drive 0.5 miles to the first stoplight. Turn right on W. Point Loma Blvd. and follow it 0.3 miles to a 4-way stop. Turn right on Bacon Street and follow that into the park. After about 0.2 miles, park on your left up against the San Diego River channel. Try different spots along the river for the best vantage points.

- **Area 2 (Sunset Cliffs)** – From **Area 1**, exit the park and turn left back onto W. Point Loma Blvd. Turn right on Sunset Cliffs Blvd. and drive south 1.4 miles to the first cliff-side parking area. Try the other parking areas as you continue southward. The parking lot closest to the breeding Brandt's Cormorants is 0.3 miles beyond the first one, close to Froude Street. Park and walk south to the stack that is just offshore.

- **Area 3 (Point Loma Neighborhoods)** – From **Area 2** drive south 0.3 miles to Hill Street. Turn left onto Hill Street and drive east 0.7 miles to Catalina Blvd. Turn right on Catalina and drive south 0.4 miles to Dudley Street. Turn left onto Dudley, drive 0.2 miles, and park at the corner of Dudley Street and Silvergate Avenue.

- **Area 4 (Nazarene University)** – From **Area 3**, return to Catalina Blvd. and turn right. Drive north 0.1 miles on Catalina Blvd. to Lomaland Drive. Turn left and drive west 0.2 miles to the college entrance.

- **Area 5 (Cabrillo National Monument)** – From **Area 4**, return to Catalina Blvd. and turn right. Drive 3.0 miles south to the entrance of Cabrillo National Monument. Immediately after driving past the entrance kiosk, go straight to visit the lighthouse, or turn right to visit the coastal cliffs and tide pools.

- **Area 6 (San Diego Bay)** – There are numerous points from which to access San Diego Bay, a few of which are listed here. Shelter Island is accessed via Shelter Island Drive. Harbor Island is accessed via N. Harbor Drive. Silver Strand Blvd. (Highway 75) and the Silver Strand beaches are accessed by driving south from the town of Coronado or north from Imperial Beach.

- **Area 7 (Quivira Basin)** – From the intersection of I-8 and I-5, drive west on I-8 for 0.3 miles to Exit 1, W. Mission Bay Drive. Drive northwest 0.7 miles (turns into Ingraham Street). Take the exit ramp loop onto W. Mission Bay Drive and drive 0.5 miles to Quivira Access Road. Turn left onto the access road and then left again onto Quivira Road. Drive 1.2 miles to the end of the road and park there, overlooking Quivira Basin.

- **Area 8 (Balboa Park)** – This large park is just north of I-5 and east of Highway 163. There are multiple access points into the park; one way to reach the park from I-5 is to take the Pershing Drive exit and drive north into the park.

- **Area 9 (Tecolote Canyon)** – From the intersection of I-5 and I-8, go north on I-5 for about 0.5 miles and exit onto Tecolote Road. Head northeast 0.7 miles on Tecolote Road to the parking lot for the nature center. Make sure you travel all the way up the road to the nature center parking lot—go past the parking lot for the Tecolote Park and Recreation Center (which has a playground behind it). Even if the nature center is closed, you can access the trail that leads into the canyon.

Site Notes

Ownership
- Federal Government (Navy, Department of the Interior)
- City of San Diego
- Private

Vehicle Access
- All roads are paved and suitable for 2-wheel drive cars

Fees
- Cabrillo National Monument (park fees)
- The San Diego Zoo charges a hefty admission price—you may wish to check your local credit union, MWR office, or other organizations for discounts before you pay full-price

Camping
- Some of the California State Park beaches have RV and tent camping

Restrooms
- Cabrillo National Monument
- Robb Field and other parks
- Restaurants and gas stations

Food
- Restaurants, groceries, and convenience stores of every ethnicity and price range abound in San Diego

Gas
- Stations throughout San Diego

Addresses
Robb Field Athletic Park
2525 Bacon Street
San Diego, CA 92107

Balboa Park
1549 El Prado
San Diego, CA 92101

Tecolote Canyon Natural Park
5180 Tecolote Road
San Diego, CA 92110

Phone Contacts
- Robb Field: (619) 224-2997
- Balboa Park: (619) 239-0512
- Tecolote Natural Canyon Park: (858) 581-9959, (858) 581-9952

Websites

http://www.sandiego.gov/park-and-recreation/centers/recctr/robb.shtml

http://www.balboapark.org/

http://www.sandiego.gov/park-and-recreation/parks/osp/tecolote/

Other Notes
- Lots of weekday rush-hour traffic throughout San Diego, so plan accordingly. And on weekends, there is also a lot of foot traffic in the parks themselves.
- Most parks have big signs that warn you to leave nothing of value in your vehicle, especially in plain sight
- Parking can be a problem in beach-front areas, especially later in the day and on weekends

---

Look for birds here:
Eucalyptus with lerps (a kind of insect) attract warblers and other insectivores.
Fruiting trees attract finches, tanagers and parrots.
Blooming trees attract insects, which in turn attract flycatchers, warblers, orioles—and hummingbirds.

B. Chula Vista Bayfront Park (J Street Mudflats)

Habitat
- Mudflats
- Open water
- Harbor
- Rocky shoreline
- Park

Target Birds
- Brant (winter)
- Scaup: Lesser and Greater (winter)
- Loons (winter)
- Other Western waterfowl (migration and winter)
- Waders (resident)
- Ridgway's Rail (resident)
- Western shorebirds (resident, migration, and winter)
- Gulls: California, Western, Herring, and Glaucous-winged (migration and winter)
- Terns: Royal and Forster's (winter); Least, Caspian, and Gull-billed (summer)
- Black Skimmer (resident)
- American Crow (resident)
- Western warblers and flycatchers (migration)

General Description
This small park is one of the better sites in the county for waterfowl, wading birds, shorebirds, gulls, and terns. Search the mudflats south of the park for a variety of breeding, migrant, and wintering shorebirds and waders. Marsh-loving birds like Savannah Sparrow and Ridgway's Rail live in the marsh year round. Scan San Diego Bay and the harbor for wintering waterfowl, including Brant, Red-throated Loon, Surf and White-winged (rare) Scoters, and Greater Scaup. During the winter some of the park visitors feed the gulls, so it's a good spot to practice your gull ID and photography skills.

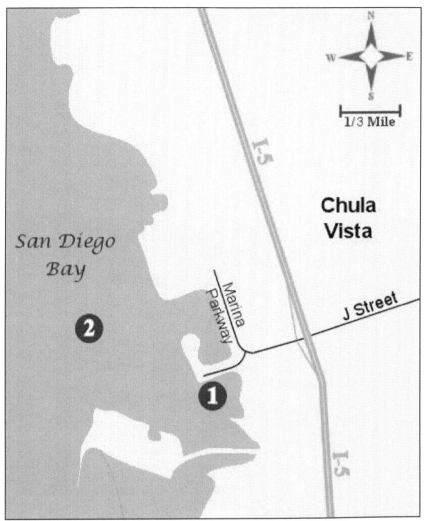

Bayfront Park (J Street Mudflats)

Birding Suggestions

1) Marsh and Mudflats

Search here from the middle of summer through spring for 14+ species of regularly visiting shorebirds, such as Black-bellied Plover, Long-billed Curlew, Marbled Godwit, and Dunlin. Also keep an eye out for less common shorebirds like Snowy Plover and Red Knot. Waterfowl congregate along the edge of the marsh at high tide. An incoming or high tide is also the best time to see Ridgway's Rail. Egrets, herons, terns, and gulls all make use of the marsh and

26

shallow water. Peregrine Falcon and Northern Harrier enjoy feeding here. Among the many American Wigeon, keep looking for the rare but regular Eurasian Wigeon.

Scope the raised berms south and west of the park for resting Black Skimmers (most common in summer), terns (year round), geese (winter), and waders (resident). During November 2015 I saw a Reddish Egret there.

2) San Diego Bay

In the winter and during migration, look in the harbor and out over the bay for Red-throated and Common Loons, five species of grebe (six if you're really lucky), Greater and Lesser Scaup, geese, and all regularly occurring western waterfowl. In winter you may count hundreds of Brant and Surf Scoters loafing in the deeper waters of the bay.

In the parking lot itself you'll find a variety of juvenile and mature gulls milling about waiting for the next park visitor to feed them some bread. In winter, look for Herring, Ring-billed, and Western Gulls. Less frequently seen are Bonaparte's, California, Glaucous-winged, and rarely even Thayer's Gulls.

Satellite view of Bayfront Park

Driving Directions to Bayfront Park

- Travel south from San Diego on I-5.
- Take exit 7B for Marina Parkway and drive west 0.3 miles to Marina Way.

27

- Turn left onto Marina Way.
- Immediately take the first left into a small parking area—this provides the best access to scan the marsh just to the south.
- Go back to Marina Way, turn left, and drive a short distance to the end of the road—which provides access to additional parking lots and bayfront viewing.

Site Notes

Best Time to Visit: Winter has the best diversity of waterfowl, waders, shorebirds, and raptors

Ownership: Unified Port of San Diego

Vehicle Access: All roads are paved and fine for 2-wheel drive

Fees: None

Camping: None

Restrooms: Two facilities in the park—one on the east side along Marina Parkway, and one on the northwest side of the parking lot next to the harbor

Food: Chula Vista

Gas: Chula Vista

Address: 980 Marina Way, Chula Vista, CA

Phone: (619) 686-6200

Web: https://www.portofsandiego.org/chula-vista-bayfront-park.html

C. Imperial Beach

Habitat
- Residential
- Ocean
- Beach
- Saltmarsh
- Salt lakes and ponds

Target Birds
- Western waterfowl (migration and winter)
- Brown Booby (increasingly common wanderer from nearby Coronado Islands)
- Bitterns: American and Least (resident)
- Night-Heron: Yellow-crowned and Black-crowned (resident)
- Reddish Egret (resident)
- Little Blue Heron (resident)
- White-tailed Kite (resident)
- Northern Harrier (winter)
- Ridgway's Rail (resident)
- Western shorebirds (migration and winter)
- Northern Fulmar and other pelagics (primarily migration and winter)
- Falcons: Prairie and Peregrine (winter)
- Western warblers and flycatchers (migration and a few in winter)
- California Towhee (resident)
- Nelson's Sparrow (rare winter)

General Description
This vibrant community of 26,000+ residents is bounded on three sides by excellent birding opportunities: the Pacific Ocean on the west; San Diego Bay to the north; and the Tijuana River Estuary to the south. Terns, gulls, shorebirds, scoters, and the occasional pelagic frequent the Pacific Ocean and the Imperial Beach shoreline, especially in the winter. The Imperial Beach Pier takes you far out into the ocean, and provides a good vantage point from which to scan for scoters and pelagics. The south end of San Diego Bay has been identified as a Globally Important Bird Area, and is one of the best sites in southern California for wading birds, shorebirds, and terns. In the marshes of the Tijuana River National

Estuarine Research Reserve you'll find Ridgway's Rails, bitterns, shorebirds, waterfowl, and sparrows.

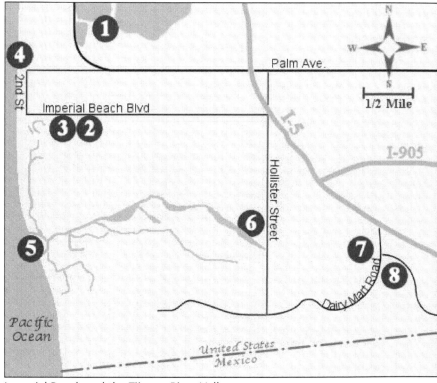

Imperial Beach and the Tijuana River Valley

Birding Suggestions

1) Salt Works Ponds

These ponds are at the southern end of the San Diego Bay and are a portion of the San Diego Bay NWR. They were formerly used by the South Bay Salt Works as evaporation ponds to produce salt. Some of the ponds are still used for that purpose today, others have been restored to marshland. At the north end of 7th Street you'll find a walking/bike path which borders the southernmost salt ponds and provides nice views of the numerous waders, shorebirds, gulls, and terns. This is one of the most reliable spots to hunt for Reddish Egret year round. Aside from the regular influx of migrating and wintering shorebirds, it's a great spot to search for Asian rarities, such as the

Lesser Sand-plover seen by hundreds of birders in July 2013. The Belding's subspecies of the Savannah Sparrow is common here. Most of the refuge is closed off to protect resident and migratory birds, but you may wish to join one of the monthly walks led by the San Diego Audubon Society.

2) Imperial Beach Sports Complex

Yellow-crowned Night-Heron

The trees in the parking area of this large sports park and in the apartment complex to the west are home to a variety of nesting waders and wintering passerines.

In all seasons look in the pines for nesting and roosting Yellow-crowned Night-Heron, a local western rarity. The nests and the birds are usually well-concealed close to the top of the trees at the western edge of the sports park; usually the "whitewash" on the ground gives them away. Most years you'll also find nesting and roosting Black-crowned Night-Heron and Snowy Egret. During winter, the large flowering trees (also along the west edge of the park) have been home to both Hepatic and Summer Tanagers, and vagrant warblers. Please park in the sports center parking lot, and be aware that the apartment complex is private property.

3) Tijuana Estuary Visitor Center

This is one of the easier places to actually see (vs. hearing) a Ridgway's (Clapper) Rail, especially during high tide. Walk the trails at all seasons and look along the creeks that slice through the marshes--if you miss it on your first visit, keep persevering. Long-billed Curlew is also common, either flying over or wandering through the marshlands. Various species of waterfowl frequent the waterways, and raptors such as White-tailed Kite hunt rodents while Peregrine Falcons hunt birds.

4) Imperial Beach Pier and Shoreline

Scoping and scanning from the vantage point of this pier during migration and winter can yield a fine array of ocean-loving species. Many unusual species for San Diego County have been spotted from here, including Long-tailed Duck, Black Scoter, and Northern Fulmar.

Camp Surf and some of the breakwaters north of the Imperial Beach Pier provide fine looks at Surfbird and other shorebirds during migration. Sanderling, plovers, turnstones, and many sandpipers are easily picked out. Pelagics and sea ducks are regularly offshore. Look for unusual wintering warblers at Camp Surf, such as Palm.

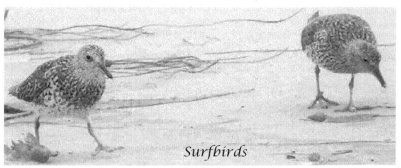

Surfbirds

5) Tijuana River Mouth

The walk from the end of Seacoast Drive (where you can park) to the river mouth can yield a plethora of bird species. Especially during high tide, you may spot resident Ridgway's Rail from Seacoast Drive. I've also seen picture-perfect American Bitterns posing here.

Peregrine Falcons and White-tailed Kites perch and hunt over the marsh. Scoters are regular offshore during winter, and often come into the estuary to feed. Pacific Loons are common migrants and winter along the coast. Snowy Plover breeds and Pacific Golden Plover is a regular winter visitor. Elegant and Royal Terns are common during summer and winter,

Snowy Plover

respectively. You may be able to get good close-up views of resting terns and gulls here—bring your camera! Keep an eye out for Reddish Egret here. Depending on the season, watch for pelagics like Parasitic Jaeger and Black-vented Shearwater. Also look out over the ocean for Brown Booby, which breeds on the Coronado Islands and often wanders to fish along the coast. This is an excellent area to scan gulls for unusual species like Mew and Glaucous-winged. Check also for vagrants, such as Belcher's Gull, which once spent a winter season here. Another rarity which returns most winters is

32

Nelson's Sparrow—these are best searched for during the highest of tides.

Sites 6 - 8

Please see next chapter for a description of these locations.

Driving Directions to Imperial Beach Locations

From San Diego take I-5 south

- **Area 1 (Salt Ponds)**
  - Take exit 5A for Palm Avenue.
  - Drive west on Palm Avenue for 1.7 miles until you reach 7th Street
  - Turn right (north) onto 7th Street, drive 0.2 miles, and park.

- **Area 2 (Sports Complex)**
  - Take exit 5A for Palm Avenue.
  - Drive west on Palm Avenue for 1.5 miles until you reach 9th Street.
  - Turn left (south) onto 9th Street and drive 0.5 miles to Imperial Beach Blvd.
  - Turn right (west) onto Imperial Beach Blvd. and drive 0.7 miles to 4th Street.
  - Turn left (south) onto 4th Street and drive 0.1 mile straight into the parking lot.

- **Area 3 (Tijuana Slough NWR Visitor Center)**
  - From **Area 2**, exit the park and immediately turn left (west) onto Caspian Way (this street is not shown on my overview map).
  - Drive west on Caspian Way for about 400 feet to the visitor center parking lot.

- **Area 4 (Tijuana River Mouth)**
  - From **Area 3**, turn left on Caspian Way and follow it 0.2 miles to Imperial Beach Blvd.
  - Turn left (west) onto Imperial Beach Blvd. and drive 0.3 miles to Seacoast Drive.
  - Turn left (south) onto Seacoast Drive and drive 0.7 miles to the end of the road; park where you can.
  - Walk south along the beach to the Tijuana River Mouth (about one mile).

- **Area 5 (Imperial Beach Pier)**
  Form the end of Seacoast Drive (**Area 4**) drive north 0.9 miles to the pier. If you can't park along the street, there is a nearby parking lot at Elkwood and Seacoast.

Site Notes

Best Times to Visit: Migration and winter are best for waterfowl, shorebirds, raptors, gulls, terns, and Nelson's Sparrow

Ownership
- City of Imperial Beach
- Department of the Interior (National Wildlife Refuges)

Vehicle Access
- Roads are paved and fine for 2-wheel drive

Fees: None

Camping: None

Restrooms
- Imperial Beach Sports Park
- Tijuana Slough NWR Visitor Center

Food: Imperial Beach

Gas: Imperial Beach

Address:
Tijuana Slough NWR Visitor Center
301 Caspian Way
Imperial Beach, CA 91932

Phone: (619) 575-2704

Websites
http://www.fws.gov/refuge/tijuana_slough/
http://www.fws.gov/refuge/San_Diego_Bay/visit/visitor_activities.html

D. Tijuana River Valley

Habitat
- Farm fields (fallow and cultivated)
- Sod and short-grass fields
- Cottonwood and willow riparian woods
- Residential
- Ponds
- Marshes

Target Birds
- Western waterfowl (migration and winter)
- Bitterns: American and Least (resident)
- White-tailed Kite (resident)
- Northern Harrier (winter)
- Red-shouldered Hawk (resident)
- Ridgway's Rail (resident)
- Plovers and other western shorebirds (migration)
- Greater Roadrunner (resident)
- Yellow-billed Cuckoo (summer)
- Hummingbirds: Anna's (resident), Allen's and Rufous (migration)
- Falcons: Prairie and Peregrine (migration and winter)
- Black-throated Magpie-Jay (exotic resident)
- Loggerhead Shrike (winter)
- "Least" Bell's Vireo (summer)
- California Thrasher (resident)
- Pipits: American (winter) and Red-throated (vagrant)
- Yellow-breasted Chat (summer) and western warblers (migration)
- Blue Grosbeak (summer)
- California Towhee (resident)
- Orioles: Bullock's and Hooded (summer)

General Description
Although this area of agriculture, horse farms, and riparian land is but a shadow of its former self, it still provides some fine recreational birding. Fortunately, with the creation of the 1800-acre Tijuana River Valley Regional Park (TRVRP), more natural habitats are being preserved. Over 22 miles of trails provide access to this area. Around Dairy Mart Ponds you'll find bitterns, waterfowl, White-tailed Kite and other raptors, and

breeding "Least" Bell's Vireo. Migration adds flycatchers and warblers, including the odd eastern vagrant. This is the best place in the U.S. to see the exotic and colorful Magpie Jay. A spring morning spent here should net you a fine list of 75 or more species.

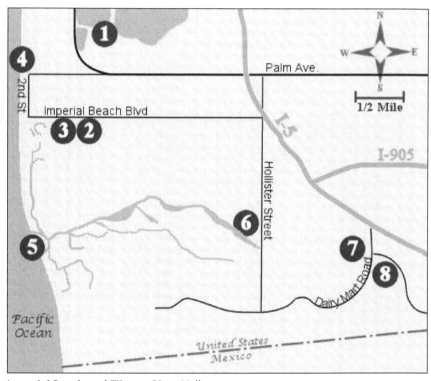

Imperial Beach and Tijuana River Valley

Birding Suggestions

Sites 1 - 5. Please see previous chapter

6) Bird and Butterfly Garden

The riparian area directly behind the small visitor center has many migrants and wintering sparrows. Yellow-breasted Chat breeds and Northern Waterthrush is a regular fall and winter vagrant. The many flowering bushes and flowers attract Allen's, Rufous, and Black-chinned Hummingbirds during migration. Warblers and flycatchers are attracted to the large athel tamarisks and other trees. Olive-sided Flycatcher is regular in the spring. Black-and-White Warbler is a

36

regular winter vagrant here. Listen and watch for the exotic Black-throated Magpie-Jay, which may be seen here and elsewhere in the Tijuana Valley. About 0.1 miles north of this area (across the bridge) is a community vegetable garden which is usually home to Cassin's Kingbird and Common Ground-Dove. Both of these locations are within the TRVRP.

7) Dairy Mart Ponds

This area is also part of the TRVPR and has several ponds of varying size and depth, mixed woodlands and riparian areas, and brushy fields. The habitat is great for all kinds of birds, and as of 2015 it boasts an eBird list of 194 species.

The largest pond is the most northerly (closest to I-5) and usually has waterfowl, herons, Common Yellowthroat, Yellow-breasted Chat (summer), Blue Grosbeak (summer), Song Sparrow, and blackbirds. In winter this is a good spot to look for gulls and terns. The smallest pond is often called "Stick" Pond, and has hosted one or more vagrant Northern Waterthrushes for several winters. This is also a good area for Solitary Sandpiper.

On the trails connecting the ponds and radiating out into the regional parklands, look for White-tailed Kite, Peregrine Falcon (winter) and other raptors, Downy and Nuttall's Woodpeckers, hummingbirds, flycatchers (summer and migration), Loggerhead Shrike, Bell's and other vireos (summer and migration), California Thrasher, warblers, California Towhee, Fox and Golden-crowned Sparrows (winter), and Lazuli Bunting (summer).

White-tailed Kite

8) Sod Farm

From the roads that circle this sod farm look in migration and winter among the hordes of Killdeer for Black-bellied and Semipalmated Plovers and, rarely, Pacific Golden-Plover. Other grass-loving visitors include Long-billed Curlew, Whimbrel, Pectoral and Baird's Sandpipers, and lots of peeps. Some of the rare shorebirds to visit these lawns have been American Golden-Plover, Ruff, Buff-breasted Sandpiper, and Upland Sandpiper. In some years you'll find vagrant Red-throated Pipit during the fall or mixed in with the regular wintering American Pipits. The odd longspur has also shown up among the pipits and Western Meadowlarks. The surrounding fields are good for resident White-tailed Kite and American Kestrel, and wintering Northern Harrier.

Driving Directions to Tijuana River Valley Locations

- **Area 6 (Bird and Butterfly Garden)**
  - Take Exit 4 from I-5 onto Hollister Street (or drive east on Coronado from Imperial Beach and turn right onto Hollister).
  - Drive south on Hollister for 1.6 miles to the parking lot for the gardens on the right (west) side of the road.

- **Area 7 (Dairy Mart Ponds)**
  - Take Exit 3 from I-5 onto Dairy Mart Road.
  - Turn right and drive west 0.2 miles on Dairy Mart Road to the first dirt parking lot area for the ponds.
  - Look at the maps on the kiosk; the largest pond is just north of the parking lot.
  - The next parking area is 0.3 miles south, and is just south of the "Stick" Pond.

- **Area 8 (Sod Farms)**
  - Take Exit 3 from I-5 onto Dairy Mart Road.
  - Turn right and drive west 0.3 miles on Dairy Mart Road to the northwest corner of the sod farms.
  - The sod farms extend for another half mile and are bordered by a decent dirt road on the west. They are bordered by a levee road on the east side, but this was off limits to private vehicles (as of 2015).

Site Notes

Best Times to Visit: With the excellent weather here along the coast, any time of year is good. However, spring will usually yield the biggest bird lists, with both residents and migrants, and a few remaining winter visitors.

Ownership
- County of San Diego
- Private

Vehicle Access
- Most roads are paved and fine for 2-wheel drive
- If you explore the area, a few of the dirt farm roads may require high clearance, especially after rains

Fees: None

Camping: None

Restrooms
- TRVRP Ranger Station
- Imperial Beach
- Chula Vista

Food: Imperial Beach and Chula Vista

Gas: Imperial Beach and Chula Vista

Address
Tijuana River Valley Regional Park Ranger Station
2721 Monument Road
San Diego, CA 92154

Phone: (619) 428-2946

Websites
http://www.sandiegocounty.gov/parks/openspace/tjrv.html
http://www.sandiegocounty.gov/reusable_components/images/parks/doc/Trails_TJRVP.pdf (Tijuana River Valley Regional Park trail map)

E. La Jolla Cove

Habitat
- Ocean
- Rocky shoreline
- Park

Target Birds
- Brown Pelican (resident)
- Brown Booby (rare, but becoming more common)
- Scoters: Surf, White-winged, and Black (migration and winter)
- Western Grebe (resident)
- Wandering Tattler (migration and winter)
- Surfbird (migration and winter)
- Black Turnstone (migration and winter)
- Cormorants: Brandt's and Double-crested (resident), and Pelagic (winter)
- Loons: Pacific, Common, and Red-throated (winter)
- Terns: Royal (winter), Elegant (summer), and Forster's (migration)
- Gulls: Heermann's, Western, Glaucous-winged (winter), and Bonaparte's (migration)
- Pelagics: Black-vented Shearwater (winter), Sooty Shearwater (summer), and other shearwaters (migration); Parasitic and other Jaegers (migration); Common Murre (migration); Cassin's and other Auklets (migration); murrelets (migration)
- Peregrine Falcon (winter)
- Anna's Hummingbird (resident)

General Description
Due to a marine trench not far offshore, this is the best location in San Diego County to look for pelagic species from shore. Depending on the season, you can scan the cove and the ocean for loons, waterfowl, boobies, shearwaters, gulls, and terns. Every year rare vagrants turn up, especially during days with winds blowing out of the west. Beware though, on some days you may not see any pelagics, and on other days they may be but dots on the horizon. The rocky shoreline has a good selection of shorebirds in migration and in winter. The cliffs hold breeding Brandt's Cormorant and Western Gull. You'll also be able to watch sea lions and harbor seals on the cliffs and in the water. The small

park has wintering Ruby-crowned Kinglet and Yellow-rumped Warbler. There is a lot of parking along Coast Blvd., but you may find it tough to find a space during the afternoons and weekends—early mornings are much easier.

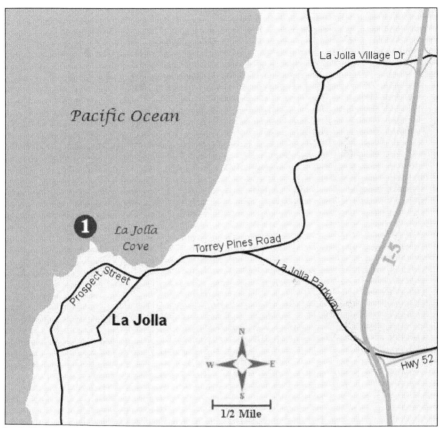

La Jolla

Birding Suggestion: La Jolla Cove and Park

A 2000-foot marine trench lies offshore of La Jolla Cove. The upwelling of nutrients and plankton provides good food for fish, which in turn draws good numbers of cormorants, gulls, terns, and pelagics. Look for both Brandt's and Pelagic Cormorants; the Brandt's breed in the La Jolla Cliffs and the Pelagic

41

Brandt's Cormorants

Cormorants visit in the winter. Just offshore you'll see mats of brownish grasses floating in the water; these are kelp beds. The kelp provides protection for fish and otters, and adds greatly to the biodiversity. Other mammals to look for in addition to otters are sea lions, harbor seals, and farther offshore, dolphins and whales.

Shorebirds
Shorebirds can be found on the cliffs, on the sandy shore of La Jolla Cove Beach, and on the rocky shoreline farther southwest at Seal Rock. Walking the seaside trail from Point La Jolla down to Seal Rock is usually productive. From the fall through the spring watch for Whimbrel, Spotted and Least Sandpipers, Willet, Black-bellied Plover, Wandering Tattler,

Whimbrel

Surfbird, and Black Turnstone. Also seen here in the past has been Black Oystercatcher, a bird that is usually easier to find at Cabrillo National Monument.

Gulls
Gulls feeding on the water and resting on the cliffs almost always include Heermann's and Western Gulls. During migration and winter these gulls are joined by Bonaparte's Gull, Herring Gull, and the occasional Glaucous-winged and Mew Gulls. Rarely Glaucous Gull and Black-legged Kittiwake make an appearance. Franklin's Gull has also been spotted here.

Heermann's Gull

Terns
During the summer months look for Elegant Tern feeding just offshore. Migration brings Forster's and Caspian Terns, and winter brings Royal Terns.

Waterfowl
During migration skeins of Pacific Loons and scoters stream by. In winter Red-throated and Common Loons feed in the surf. Western Grebe often feeds in and beyond the kelp beds during migration.

Pelagics
These are birds of the vast ocean and usually only come within sight of land when the winds push them eastward. Most of the sea watches are done from the farthest northwest point of the park. Often you'll have to look west beyond the kelp beds to see the pelagic birds, but if conditions are right they'll come closer, sometimes even into the cove itself. During the summer months the most commonly sighted pelagic is Sooty Shearwater. During other times of the year look for Black-vented Shearwater. Less common, but regularly sighted during migration are phalaropes, Common Murre, Northern Fulmar, skuas, jaegers, other shearwaters, and auklets. During summer look for Black and other Storm-Petrels.

Extras
Brown Pelican also breeds on the cliffs and feeds in La Jolla Cove. Brown Boobies are rare but regular visitors; Masked and Nazca Boobies have been spotted over the years, but are very rare vagrants. If you're really lucky, you might catch sight of a Red-billed Tropicbird. Black Phoebe, Anna's Hummingbird, American Crow, and Song Sparrow are regulars in the small park which sits atop La Jolla Cliffs. During winter watch for other sparrows and patrolling Peregrine Falcons.

Driving Directions to La Jolla Cove
- From San Diego drive north on I-5 and take exit 26A for La Jolla Parkway.
- Drive west on La Jolla Parkway for 4.7 miles (La Jolla Parkway becomes Torrey Pines Road).
- At 4.7 miles turn left (north) on Prospect Place.
- Drive north on Prospect Place for 0.2 miles to Coast Blvd.
- Turn right (north) onto Coast Blvd. and look for a parking spot as you drive downhill. (The farther downhill you can drive and park, the less you'll have to walk. But, if you can't find any parking farther down the hill, you'll have to circle all the way around to get back to that parking spot you passed by!) The cliffs will be in front of you as you park, and the cove is directly in front of these cliffs (which host the breeding Brandt's Cormorants). Walk north past the lifeguard station and La Jolla

43

Cove Beach to Point La Jolla, regarded as the best sea watch (pelagic) vantage point.
- To return to I-5 northbound, take Prospect Street to Torrey Pines Road north to La Jolla Village Drive and follow the signs to I-5.

Site Notes

Best Times to Visit
- Fall migration is best for most pelagics
- Winter is good for waterfowl, shorebirds, and some of the pelagics

Ownership: City of La Jolla

Vehicle Access: Paved roads and parking lots are all good for any kind of vehicle

Fees: Parking at La Jolla Cove is free

Camping: None

Restrooms: In the park next to La Jolla Cove

Food: La Jolla

Gas: La Jolla

Wandering Tattler

F. San Elijo Lagoon

Habitat
- Tidal estuary
- Riparian woodlands
- Coastal sage scrub
- Chaparral

Target Birds
- Teal: Green-winged, Cinnamon, and Blue-winged (winter)
- Other western waterfowl (migration and winter)
- Bitterns: American and Least (resident)
- Osprey
- White-tailed Kite
- Northern Harrier (winter)
- Ridgway's Rail (resident)
- Western shorebirds (migration)
- Terns: Royal (winter), Elegant (summer), and Forster's (winter)
- Hummingbirds: Anna's and Allen's (resident), and Rufous (migration)
- Nuttall's Woodpecker (resident)
- Falcons: Merlin, Prairie, and Peregrine (migration and winter)
- Loggerhead Shrike (winter)
- Wrens: House, Marsh, and Bewick's (resident)
- California Gnatcatcher (resident)
- Wrentit (resident)
- California Thrasher (resident)
- Western warblers and flycatchers (migration)
- Blue Grosbeak (summer)
- California Towhee (resident)
- Sparrows: Song, Savannah (Belding's), Fox, White-crowned, Chipping, Golden-crowned, and Brewer's (winter and resident)

General Description
San Elijo Lagoon is a well-preserved tidal estuary surrounded by riparian scrub, coastal chaparral, and coastal strand. It covers almost 1000 acres and is one of the county's largest wetlands. An astounding 40% of U.S. birds have been spotted in the preserve. There are two main access roads to this park. The south part of the preserve is reached from the north end

of N. Rios Avenue (a dead end). From here you can take one trail downhill northwest to the head of the lagoon to search for shorebirds and waterfowl, or take the other trail downhill east to search for chaparral species. The north portion of the reserve is accessed from the visitor center off of Manchester Avenue. Most weekends you can take hikes from this location led by naturalist rangers.

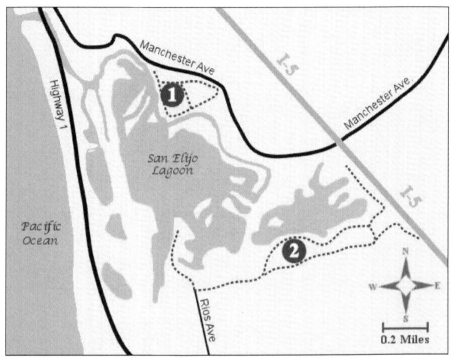

San Elijo Lagoon

Birding Suggestions

1) San Elijo Nature Center and Trails

The visitor center has a wealth of natural history exhibits and literature. A nice loop trail starts there which takes you along the marsh and then through a swampy woodlot. Look for resident Ridgway's Rail and Savannah Sparrow in the marshes, and breeding Yellow Warbler in the woods. Resident California Gnatcatcher is found here on occasion, but it isn't as easy to see as on the south side of the lagoon. During the fall of 2015 a Long-eared Owl made the woods home for a short while. Migration brings all varieties of

46

western flycatchers and warblers. During winter you'll find three species of teal and numerous other waterfowl.

2) N. Rios Avenue Trails

As you take the trail leading downhill from the end of N. Rios Avenue to the northwest (towards the ocean), listen and watch for resident Wrentits and wintering Fox and Golden-crowned Sparrows, which find cover in the low chaparral brush. As you approach the salt marsh look for resident Song and Savannah Sparrows. At the end of the trail, set up a scope and look through the mass of gulls, terns, waders, and shorebirds (especially in migration and winter). Depending on the season, you may find Elegant, Royal, and Forster's Terns, a variety of gulls, and a plethora of waterfowl and shorebirds.

California Gnatcatcher

The trail leading down the hill to the northeast takes you next to and through chaparral habitat, which is good for resident Western Scrub-Jay, California Thrasher, Spotted Towhee, and Wrentit. After a quarter of a mile you'll start seeing beavertail cacti, which lets you know you've entered the scrubland which is prime habitat for the endangered, resident California Gnatcatcher. Spring is a good time to hunt for these tiny birds, when they are most likely to "sing." As you hunt for the gnatcatchers, watch also for resident Allen's and Anna's Hummingbirds, and migrating Rufous Hummingbirds. Every once in a while this trail can be alive with Wrentits, and will offer unparalleled opportunities to take photos of these normally secretive birds. In winter, watch the tree tops and the sky for Peregrine Falcon, which hunt the numerous species of shorebirds.

Driving Directions to San Elijo Lagoon

San Elijo Lagoon is about 20 miles north of San Diego, just off the I-5. From the intersection of the I-5 and the I-8:

- **Area 1 (San Elijo Nature Center and Trails)**
  - Drive 18.7 miles north on I-5 from the intersection of I-8 and I-5.

- Exit onto Manchester Avenue and drive west 0.7 miles to the entrance for the visitor center.
- **Area 2 (N. Rios Avenue Trails)**
  - Drive 17.0 miles north on I-5 from the intersection of I-8 and I-5.
  - Take exit 37 onto Lomas Santa Fe Drive (towards Solano Beach).
  - Drive west 0.9 miles on Lomas Santa Fe Drive to N. Rios Avenue.
  - Turn right onto N. Rios Avenue and drive north 0.8 miles to the dead end, where you can park along the road.

Site Notes

Best Times to Visit
- Spring is best for the California Gnatcatchers, which are actively singing at this time of year
- Migration is great for warblers and shorebirds
- Winter is best for raptors and waterfowl

Ownership: County of San Diego

Vehicle Access: Paved roads and parking lots

Fees: None

Hours: San Elijo Nature Center open 9:00 a.m. – 5:00 p.m. daily

Camping: None

Restrooms
- San Elijo Nature Center
- Surrounding gas stations in Solano Beach

Food: Solano Beach

Gas: Solano Beach

Address
San Elijo Nature Center
2710 Manchester Avenue
Cardiff-by-the-Sea, CA 92007

Phone number: (760) 634-3026

Websites
http://www.fws.gov/refuge/tijuana_slough/
http://www.sanelijo.org/welcome-san-elijo-lagoon-conservancy

G. Guajome Regional Park

Habitat
- Riparian woods
- Ponds
- Marsh
- Chaparral
- Mixed grasslands

Target Birds
- Teal: Green-winged, Cinnamon, and Blue-winged (winter)
- Other western waterfowl (migration and winter)
- Hawks: Red-tailed (resident), Cooper's, Sharp-shinned (winter)
- Hummingbirds: Anna's, Allen's, Black-chinned, and Rufous (resident and migration)
- Woodpeckers: Nuttall's and Downy (resident), Acorn and Northern Flicker (winter)
- Sapsuckers: Red-naped and Red-breasted (winter)
- Bell's Vireo (summer)
- Western Scrub-Jay (resident)
- Bushtit (resident)
- Wrens: House and Bewick's (resident)
- California Thrasher (resident)
- Western warblers and flycatchers (migration)
- Blue Grosbeak (summer)
- California Towhee (resident)
- Goldfinches: American and Lesser (resident)

General Description
This 557-acre park is about 40 miles north of San Diego. In addition to birding, you can bike, ride horses, fish, and camp. The diversity of habitats here has led to a list of 186+ observed bird species. Over four miles of trails provide access to a fine marsh, a 25-acre lake, a small pond, woodlands, a bit of chaparral, and grasslands. Many of the common chaparral and woodland birds are found here, including a variety of woodpeckers, thrashers, towhees, and finches. You might also get lucky and see a long-tailed weasel or a bobcat.

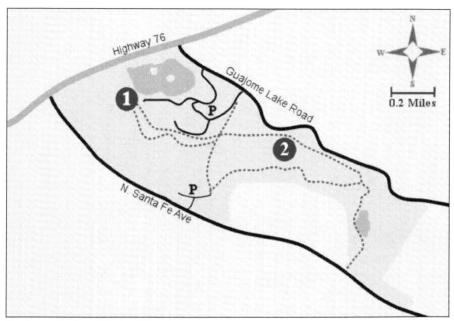

Guajome Regional Park, P-Parking

Birding Suggestions

1) Marsh and Lake

Pied-billed and both Clark's and Western Grebes may be found in the lake throughout the year. During winter a variety of waterfowl join them, such as Redhead and Hooded Merganser. In the extensive cattail and sedge habitat look for Black-crowned Night-Heron, Marsh Wren, Common Yellowthroat, and Song Sparrow. Less common are rails and Least Bittern.

In the adjacent woods, both Downy and Nuttall's Woodpeckers breed in the park, and they are usually joined in winter by Red-naped and Red-breasted Sapsuckers. "Least" Bell's Vireo is a summer resident. Among the wintering Orange-crowned, Nashville, Black-throated Gray, and Yellow-rumped Warblers, keep an eye out for vagrant American Redstart, and both Black-and-White and Black-throated Green Warblers. Orioles here are Hooded and Bullock's.

2) Trail to Upper Pond

The trail to the upper pond follows a riparian corridor and passes through brush and grasslands. Listen and watch for Western Scrub-Jay, Bushtit, California Thrasher, Wrentit, and California Towhee.

As in other parks, Song, White-crowned, and Chipping are the most common wintering sparrows, but look also for Lincoln's, Clay-colored, and Golden-crowned. Watch for American Goldfinch among the more common Lesser Goldfinches.

Driving Directions to Guajome Regional Park

From Oceanside take Highway 76 for 7.0 miles northeast to the park.

-   **Area 1 (Marsh and Lake)**
    - From Highway 76 exit right onto Guajome Lake Road.
    - Follow this road for 0.1 miles to the well-signed park entrance road and turn right.
    - Drive 0.2 miles to the parking lot for the nature trail.
-   **Area 2 (Upper Pond)**
    - From Highway 76 exit right onto N. Santa Fe Drive (S14).
    - Follow N. Santa Fe Drive for 0.6 miles to the lower picnic park entrance.
    - Turn left into the park and drive a few hundred feet to the parking area.
    - To the right (northeast) is access to the Willow Trail, which takes you to the pond.

Site Notes

Best Time to Visit: Spring migration offers the greatest variety of bird life

Ownership: San Diego County

Vehicle Access: Paved roads

Fees: Day-use fee is $3.00, camping fee is $29.00

Hours: Day use is 9:30 a.m. to sunset (or 5:00 p.m., pay attention to the signs)

Camping: 33 camp sites

Restrooms: In the park

Food: Oceanside

Gas: Oceanside

Address
Guajome Regional Park
3000 Guajome Lake Road
Oceanside, CA 92057

Phone: 760-724-4489

Website
www.sandiegocounty.gov/content/sdc/parks/Camping/guajome.html

H. Palomar Mountain

Habitat
- Pine, fir, and cedar forest
- Montane chaparral
- Riparian valleys
- Mountain meadows

Target Birds
- Hawks: Red-tailed and Red-shouldered (resident)
- Golden Eagle (resident)
- Quail: Mountain and California (resident)
- Wild Turkey (resident)
- Band-tailed Pigeon (summer)
- Owls: Flammulated (summer), Spotted (resident) and Northern Saw-whet (winter)
- Hummingbirds: Rufous and Allen's (migration)
- Woodpeckers: Nuttall's, Acorn, and Hairy (all resident)
- Red-breasted Sapsucker (resident)
- Western Wood-Pewee (summer)
- Flycatchers: Olive-sided (migrant) and Pacific-slope (summer)
- Loggerhead Shrike (winter)
- Vireos: Hutton's (resident) and Cassin's (summer)
- Violet-green Swallow (summer)
- Mountain Chickadee (resident)
- Oak Titmouse (resident)
- Nuthatches: White-breasted, Red-breasted, and Pygmy (all resident)
- Brown Creeper (resident)
- House Wren (resident)
- Bewick's Wren (resident)
- Western Bluebird (resident)
- American Robin (resident)
- California Thrasher (resident)
- Western warblers and flycatchers (migration)
- Spotted Towhee (resident)
- Dark-eyed Junco (resident)
- Western Tanager (migration)
- Black-headed Grosbeak (summer)
- Purple Finch (winter)

General Description

Palomar Mountain is a wonderful state park with 1862 acres of forest habitat in the form of Coulter and yellow pines, and giant red cedars. It is one of the higher parks in San Diego County (average elevation is 5000 ft), and consequently has high-elevation birds that are hard to find elsewhere in the county, such as Mountain Quail, Red-breasted Sapsucker, Violet-green Swallow, and Townsend's Solitaire. Keep an eye out for Lawrence's Goldfinch during the spring and summer, among the much more common Lessers. Along some of the trails you may even find banana slugs, lemon lilies, and tiger lilies. Just to the east of the park is the 6100 ft Palomar Mountain peak and the Palomar Observatory. This road to the observatory is also a fine birding destination, and in both 2012 and 2013 birders located Flammulated Owl in late May and June. Be prepared for cold weather in the winter.

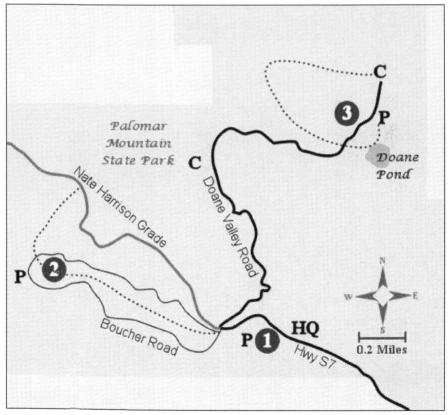

Palomar Mountain State Park — **P**-Parking **C**-Campground **HQ**-Headquarters

Birding Suggestions

All of these areas will take you through fine habitat, home to almost all the montane species of southern California.

1) Silvercrest Picnic Area

Here you'll find several huge incense cedars and oak trees. In November 2015 I birded this area and the forest around the entrance headquarters; pishing brought in no less than 15 species within a few minutes, including Steller's Jay, Oak Titmouse, Mountain Chickadee, Western Bluebird, Hermit Thrush, Townsend's Warbler, Spotted and California Towhees, and Purple Finch.

2) Boucher Trail

As you take this 3.6-mile trail leading downhill to the northwest, listen and watch for Golden Eagle (rare), White-throated Swift, Violet-green Swallow, hummingbirds, Steller's Jay, and Spotted Towhee. Fox Sparrow is often in the brush.

3) Doane Creek Trail

Band-tailed Pigeon

This 0.75-mile trail is accessible from the Doane Pond parking area. The open meadow near lower Doane Creek sometimes has Purple Martins.

Mountain Quail, Band-tailed Pigeon, Hairy Woodpecker, Red-breasted Nuthatch, Brown Creeper, Mountain Chickadee, and Dark-eyed Junco are some of the montane birds that nest here. This is also one of the few places in the county that you may find breeding Cassin's Vireo. In the past, White-headed Woodpecker was also a breeder, but there have been no recent reports. In some winters the woodpecker clan is augmented by Lewis's Woodpecker and Williamson's Sapsucker.

Flycatchers found in this park during spring and summer include Ash-throated, Dusky, Pacific-slope, Black Phoebe, and Western Wood-Pewee.

54

Driving Directions to Palomar Mountain Park

The park is about two hours from Mission Valley. From San Diego drive north about 47 miles on I-15:

- Exit onto 76 East.
- Drive 20.5 miles on Highway 76 until you come to a turnoff on your left called Palomar Mountain Road (also called S6 or South Grade Road).
- Drive up the mountain for 6.7 miles until you come to a stop sign.
- Turn left and continue for a few yards. Ahead on your left you'll see a general store and a restaurant; turn left onto the road just before the general store – this is State Park Road.
- Drive west for 3.0 miles on State Park Road to the park entrance/boundary. You'll come to a stop sign and a small building on your right—pay your entrance fee here at the park HQ, or use the self-registration envelopes if nobody is present. The birding areas are easily located by following the main road.

Site Notes

Best Times to Visit

- All seasons are good, but spring is the time with the highest diversity. This is the easiest time to find Mountain Quail, when they are calling. Migrants and winter visitors are still passing through. Breeders have returned and bird songs fill the air.
- This is also a fine inland spot to visit in the early summer, when the breeders are still singing and the surrounding inland areas are baking in the hot sun

Ownership: State

Vehicle Access: Roads are paved

Fees: Day use is $8.00 per vehicle

Hours: Day use from 8:00 a.m. to sunset

Camping

- The surrounding Cleveland National Forest has primitive camping (no fee) and developed sites (fee)
- State park has developed camping sites (fee)

Restrooms: Picnic and camping areas

Food: Valley Center

Gas: Valley Center (expensive)

Address
Palomar Mountain State Park
19952 State Park Rd.
Palomar CA 92060
Phone: 760-742-3462
Websites
http://www.parks.ca.gov/?page_id=637
http://www.palomarsp.org/
Other notes: Dogs and mountain bikes prohibited in the park

The Warblers of San Diego County Mountain Parks

Hermit – uncommon migrant that favors spruce and firs; during migration often in lower elevations, too; in the desert they often frequent athel tamarisks

Townsend's – common migrant in pines and other trees

Black-throated Gray – common migrant and breeder, favors oaks on breeding grounds

Wilson's – most often seen in riparian areas, but may be found anywhere – the most common of our migrants

MacGillivray's – a fairly common but retiring warbler of thick brushy areas; only infrequently seen in trees

Common Yellowthroat – common breeder in wet areas, like the marshes and brush around Lake Cuyamaca

Yellow – common breeder in riparian areas

Yellow-rumped – common winter visitor and migrant in many wooded areas and urban neighborhoods

Nashville – common migrant in riparian areas

Orange-crowned – common migrant and less common winter visitor in riparian areas

---

I. Lake Henshaw and Mesa Grande Road

Habitat
- Open water
- Shoreline
- Marshes
- Riparian streams
- Oak woodlands
- Mountain chaparral
- Grasslands

Target Birds
- Grebes: Western, Clark's, and Eared (resident and winter)
- Western waterfowl (mostly winter)
- Ferruginous Hawk (winter)
- Gulls: Bonaparte's, Ring-billed, and California (migration and winter)
- Terns: Caspian and Forster's (migration)
- Belted Kingfisher (winter)
- Lewis's Woodpecker (rare winter)
- Red-breasted Sapsucker (winter)
- Falcons: Peregrine and Prairie (winter)
- Willow Flycatcher (migration and summer)
- Swallows (migration and summer)
- Bluebirds: Western and Mountain (winter)
- Sparrows: Lark, Fox, Dark-eyed Junco, and Savannah (winter)

General Description
Lake Henshaw is fed by the San Luis Rey River, which itself creates great habitat on the northernmost corner of the lake. The lake is 1140 acres and is managed by the Vista Irrigation District for agriculture. Due to its large size and shallow shoreline it's a great spot to search for a variety of waterfowl, waders, shorebirds, gulls and terns. Each year brings rarities, and multiple trips increase your chances for finding something new.

The scenic, 12-mile-long Mesa Grande Road takes you through rolling countryside made up of chaparral, scattered oak groves, grassland, and farms. All seasons are good, but winter may be the best for searching out less common species like Prairie Falcon, Ferruginous Hawk, Lewis's

Woodpecker, and Mountain Bluebird. A variety of sparrows also winters in the grasslands.

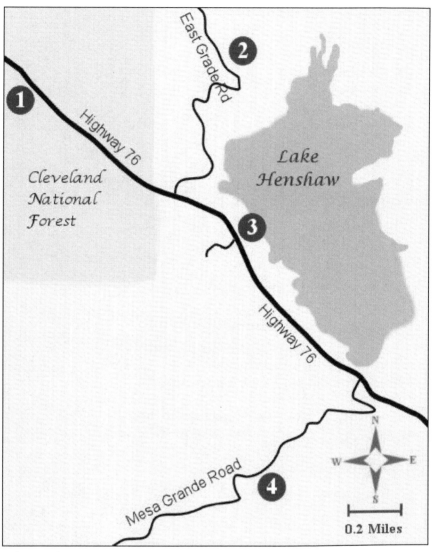

Lake Henshaw Area

Birding Suggestions

1) **San Luis Rey River Picnic Area**

Situated in the Cleveland National Forest, this cool, wooded valley along the San Luis Rey River is a great place to have a picnic and do some birding. "Southwestern Willow" Flycatchers breed here in the riparian zone, as do more common species like Nuttall's Woodpecker, Bewick's Wren, and Oak Titmouse. In winter you can find Hermit Thrush, Lincoln's Sparrow, and flocks of Dark-eyed Junco. Migrants include a fine array of western warblers, vireos, flycatchers, tanagers, and grosbeaks.

2) Lake Henshaw Scenic Overlook

From this overlook you get a distant wide-angle view of the San Luis Rey River as it winds through the valley and creates a nice delta on the north end of Lake Henshaw. This area is great for pelicans, geese, and cormorants. It is also good for shorebirds, waders, and gulls, but even with a scope all but the largest birds are pretty much un-identifiable. Easier to see are the raptors which hunt over the river, the riparian woods, and the grasslands. White-tailed Kite, Red-tailed Hawk, and Peregrine Falcon are seen in the fall, and Bald Eagle breeds in the area.

3) Lake Henshaw

This large lake has great numbers of grebes, waterfowl, waders, pelicans, gulls, terns, and shorebirds. Every season has something to offer. Falcons and other raptors ply the shoreline and interior. In migration, look for Violet-green Swallow and Vaux's Swift. From the entry gate (get the access code across the road at the Lake Henshaw Resort restaurant and convenience store) you can follow the main road down to the boat launch and picnic areas, or take one of the dirt roads that heads southeast along the lake shore. A bit of hiking takes you to the northeast corner, which has the best habitat and the highest density of species. If you're ambitious, you can also hike and bird the entire 5-mile lake perimeter.

4) Mesa Grande Road

In the winter, watch the pastures and grasslands for Ferruginous Hawk, Prairie Falcon, Western and Mountain Bluebirds, and a variety of sparrows. Lewis's Woodpecker sometimes comes down to visit these lower elevations in winter; once you locate a single bird or a small family, they usually spend

Lewis's Woodpecker

the entire season in the same locale. Look for them "flycatching" from telephone poles and perches on oak trees. They look remarkably like an American Crow when they fly. Blue Grosbeak breeds here, and Tricolored Blackbird visits the farms to feed in the fields.

Driving Directions to Lake Henshaw and Mesa Grande Road

- **Area 1 (San Luis Rey River)** – From the intersection of Palomar Mountain Road and Highway 76 drive southeast on Highway 76 for 7.8 miles to a sign marking the picnic area. Turn right into the picnic area and follow it downhill and around a sharp bend to the end, where you can park.

- **Area 2 (Lake Henshaw Scenic Overlook)** – From **Area 1**, turn right onto Highway 76 and drive southeast for 1.7 miles to East Grade Road (S7). Turn left onto S7 and drive north for 1.8 miles to the scenic overlook.

- **Area 3 (Lake Henshaw)** – From I-15 take exit 46 for Highway 76. Turn right on Highway 76 and drive east for 31.2 miles to the Lake Henshaw Resort. Get the gate access code here. Cross the highway and take the access road, enter the gate code, and proceed to the boat launch area.

- **Area 4 (Mesa Grande Road)** – From **Area 3**, turn left onto Highway 76 and drive southeast for 1.8 miles to Mesa Grande Road. Turn right on Mesa Grande Road and follow it 12 miles until it ends at Highway 79, stopping where it's safe to do so, when you see good habitat and birds.

Mountain Bluebird

Site Notes

Best Time to Visit: Winter is the time for waterfowl, raptors, woodpeckers, and sparrows
Ownership
- Private

- Vista Irrigation District
- Federal Government (Cleveland National Forest)

Vehicle Access: Most roads are paved; passenger car is fine

Fees: Day-use fee of $7 for Lake Henshaw (tell them you're birding and you might get in for free)

Restrooms
- Lake Henshaw Resort
- Boat launch/picnic area

Camping
- Lake Henshaw Resort ($20 per vehicle for camping; $25 for RV hookup; $64+ for cabins)
  http://www.lakehenshawresort.com/
  760-782-3501
- Primitive camping allowed in Cleveland National Forest just to the west of Lake Henshaw (no fee)

Food
- The Round Up Grill is across from the lake at the Lake Henshaw Resort; the sign says that they serve breakfast, lunch, and dinner
- Santa Ysabel has several options, including the "famous" Julian Pie Shop

Gas
- Santa Ysabel, 11 miles southeast of Lake Henshaw

J. Julian and William Heise County Park

Habitat
- Neighborhoods
- Parkland
- Pine and oak forests
- Chaparral
- Orchards
- Meadows
- Farmland

Target Birds
- Quail: Mountain and California (resident)
- Red-shouldered Hawk (resident)
- Owls: Western Screech-Owl and Spotted (resident)
- Belted Kingfisher (winter)
- Woodpeckers: Acorn and Nuttall's (resident)
- Jays: Steller's and Western Scrub-Jay (resident)
- Phoebes: Black and Say's (resident)
- Loggerhead Shrike (winter)
- Western swallows (migrants and resident)
- Nuthatches: Pygmy and White-breasted (resident)
- Mountain Chickadee (resident)
- Oak Titmouse (resident)
- Western Bluebird (resident)
- California Thrasher (resident)
- Phainopepla (spring)
- Western warblers (mostly migrants)
- Towhees: Spotted and California (resident), Green-tailed (winter)
- Sparrows: Song (resident) Chipping, Brewer's, Savannah, White-crowned (winter)
- Orioles: Scott's and Bullock's (summer)
- Goldfinches: Lesser (resident) and Lawrence's (irruptive)

General Description
Julian is a pleasant tourist destination high up in the Laguna Mountains. Especially during the summer, weekends can be very crowded, when hordes of tourists drive up to escape the heat and eat homemade apple pie and ice cream. The best time to bird this area on weekends is early in

the morning; weekdays are much less crowded. Southeast of Julian, William Heise County Park covers 900+ acres at an elevation of 4420 ft. Eleven miles of trails take you through red cedars, pines, and oaks. Banner Grade is a windy road that takes you from 4200 ft to 2600 ft and provides opportunities to bird the pines, chaparral, oaks, riparian woodland, the high desert.

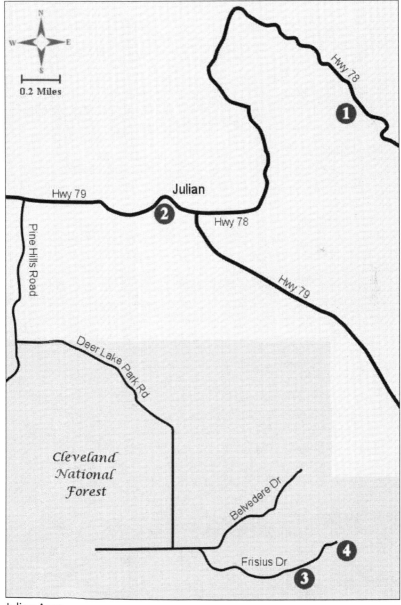

Julian Area

Birding Suggestions

1) Banner Grade

If approaching Julian from the east, Banner Grade is a stretch of Highway 78 that ascends 4.0 miles from the desert floor to the pine forests of Julian. Along the drive you'll pass through Live Oaks which are home to Acorn Woodpecker, Western Scrub-Jay, and Oak Titmouse. Mountainside chaparral is the predominant vegetation along much of the ascent; stop at pull-offs here to look and listen for resident California Quail, Wrentit, Oak Titmouse, Spotted Towhee, and California Thrasher. Winter brings Fox and White-crowned Sparrows. Once you reach the pines you'll be in the home of breeding Mountain Chickadee, Black-headed Grosbeak, Pygmy and White-breasted Nuthatch, and Steller's Jay.

2) The Birdwatcher

This large store in Julian sells gifts, publications, optics, bird feeders, and bird food. On the outside you'll find hummingbird feeders hanging from the eves and seed feeders out back. Hummingbirds to look for in migration include Rufous, Calliope, and Black-chinned. Look for Anna's all year round. Visitors to the seed feeders include Black-headed Grosbeak, Pine Siskin (winter), nuthatches, and finches. Several years ago a vagrant Common Redpoll drew in hordes of birders!

3) William Heise County Park – Cedar Trail

At Picnic Area 2 park near the restrooms and take the downhill trail which intersects with the Cedar Trail. This trail winds through beautiful red cedar and then goes up into the sunlit mountain chaparral. In the cedar forest look for Spotted Owl (at times they're easy to see, at other times they seem to be invisible). Other birds in the forest include American Robin, Brown Creeper, House Wren, Hairy Woodpecker, Dark-eyed Junco, and Spotted Towhee. As the trail ascends into the chaparral watch for resident Bushtit, Wrentit, and California Thrasher.

Wrentit

4) William Heise County Park – Group Campground

The campground host has an excellent bird-feeding station as of July 2015. At that time we spotted scores of migrant Rufous Hummingbirds there, as well as Dark-eyed Junco, Oak Titmouse, Mountain Chickadee, and Western Bluebird.

Warblers of San Diego County Mountains

Hermit – uncommon migrant that favors spruce and firs

Townsend's – common migrant in pines

Black-throated Gray – common migrant and breeder, favors oaks

Wilson's – most often seen in riparian areas, but may be found anywhere – the most common of our migrants

MacGillivray's – a fairly common but retiring warbler of thick brushy areas

Common Yellowthroat – common breeder in wet areas, like the marshes and brush around Lake Cuyamaca

Yellow – common breeder in riparian areas

Yellow-rumped – common winter visitor and migrant in many wooded areas and urban neighborhoods

Nashville – common migrant in riparian areas

Orange-crowned – common migrant and less common winter visitor in riparian areas

---

Driving Directions to Julian Birding Areas

- **Area 1 (Banner Grade)** – If you approach Julian from the east on Highway 78, you'll start ascending Banner Grade 6.2 miles east of town. If you are heading east out of Julian and will be descending the Banner Grade, drive east on Highway 78 for 2.2 miles beyond the intersection of Highways 78 and 79 to begin the 4-mile downhill drive.

- **Area 2 (The Birdwatcher)** – At the intersection of Highway 79 and Highway 78 (Main Street), drive west on Main Street for 0.2 miles to B Street. Turn left onto B Street and drive southwest up the street several hundred feet to the Birdwatcher. Turn into the parking lot and park.

- **Area 3 (William Heise County Park - Trail)**
    - From the corner of Main and Washington Streets, turn left and drive southwest on Highway 78 (Washington Street) for 0.9 miles to Pine Hills Road
    - Turn left (south) onto Pine Hills and drive 1.0 miles to Deer Lake Park Road
    - Turn left (east) onto Deer Lake Park Road and drive 2.1 miles to Frisius Drive.
    - Turn left (east) onto Frisius Drive and drive 0.5 miles into the park; pay the day use fee at the kiosk.
    - Drive 0.4 miles past the entrance kiosk to Picnic Area 2. The Cedar Trail is accessed from the south end of the picnic area.
- **Area 4 (William Heise County Park, Group Campground)** – From the entrance kiosk continue east for 0.6 miles on the main park road to the group campground. The host's trailer is at the beginning of the campground loop road.

Site Notes

Best Time to Visit: April has singing residents and numerous migrant passerines

Ownership
- San Diego County
- Private

Vehicle Access: All paved roads

Fees: William Heise County Park
- Day use is $4 per vehicle
- Camping fee depends on the type of site—varies from $24 (tent) to $62 (cabin)

Hours: William Heise County Park
- 9:30 a.m. to 5:00 p.m. on weekdays
- 9:30 a.m. to sunset on weekends

Camping: William Heise County Park has 103 developed sites and 14 cabins

Restrooms: In the park

Food: Julian

Gas: Julian

Addresses

William Heise County Park
4945 Heise Park Road
Julian, CA 92036

The Birdwatcher
2775 B Street
Julian, CA 92036

Phone: (760) 765-0650
Website: http://www.sandiegocounty.gov/parks/Camping/heise.html

K. Cuyamaca Rancho State Park

Habitat
- Riparian
- Mountains
- Oak and pine forests
- Marshes
- Open water
- Meadows
- Chaparral

Target Birds
- Grebes: Western and Clark's (winter)
- Quail: Mountain and California (resident)
- Northern Harrier (winter)
- Red-shouldered Hawk (resident)
- Owls: Western Screech-Owl and Spotted (resident)
- Woodpeckers: Hairy, Acorn and Nuttall's (resident)
- Sapsuckers: Red-naped, Red-breasted, and Williamson's (winter)
- Phoebes: Black and Say's (resident)
- Loggerhead Shrike (winter)
- Western swallows (migrants and resident)
- Jays: Steller's and Western Scrub-Jay (resident)
- Nuthatches: Pygmy and White-breasted (resident)
- Mountain Chickadee (resident)
- Oak Titmouse (resident)
- Phainopepla (spring)
- California Thrasher (resident)
- Western Bluebird (resident)
- Western warblers (mostly migration)
- Towhees: Spotted and California (resident)
- Sparrows: Song (resident) Chipping, Brewer's, Savannah, White-crowned (winter)
- Orioles: Scott's and Bullock's (summer)
- Tricolored Blackbird (irruptive, usually in summer)
- Goldfinches: Lesser (resident) and Lawrence's (irruptive)
- Finches: Cassin's and Purple (irruptive)

General Description

This 24,700-acre mountain park has great habitat variety and a multitude of birds. In 2003 the Cedar Fire burned 98% of the forest covering this park; reforestation has been taking place since then. Canyons, mountain tops (Cuyumaca Peak is 6512 ft), oak woodlands, pines, streams, grasslands, and an adjoining lake provide an abundance of hiking and birding opportunities. This is an excellent spot to look for quail, woodpeckers, flycatchers, vireos, warblers, Western Tanager, and Black-headed Grosbeak.

Winter brings waterfowl, three species of sapsuckers, kinglets, and sparrows. A hundred miles of trails make it easy to cover this park.

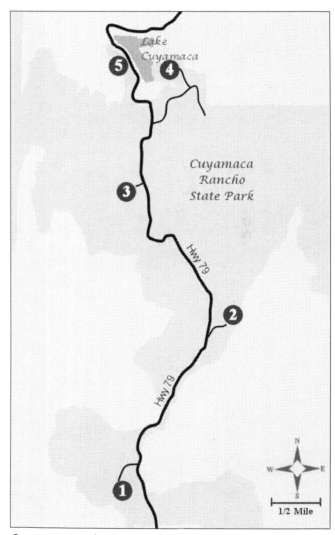

Cuyamaca Rancho State Park

Birding Suggestions

1) Green Valley Falls

This is a great scenic trail from which to bird. It's best not to try it on a warm summer's weekend, though, unless you want to share the trail and stream with scores of families coming up to escape the lowland heat. The canyon walls reverberate with the calls of Rock Wrens and the odd Canyon Wren. In the oak woodlands around the picnic area look for Western Scrub-Jay, Oak Titmouse, Hutton's Vireo, and in winter, Golden-crowned Sparrow. The creek and the riparian woods are great for Black Phoebe, joined in migration by other flycatchers, vireos, and warblers.

2) Cold Stream Trail and Visitor Center

On the hillsides above the visitor center listen and watch for both California and Mountain Quail—it's really helpful to know their very different calls. Early spring is the best time to hear the "quark" call of the Mountain Quail. A trail follows Cold Stream north and to the west of the visitor center. It is home to dozens of Acorn Woodpeckers, along with lesser numbers of Nuttall's and Hairy Woodpeckers. In the meadows to the west of the visitor center and Cold Stream look for Wild Turkey and Western Bluebird.

3) Paso Picacho Campground

This is a consistently outstanding birding location in the Laguna Mountains, an excellent spot to find most of the high-altitude breeders, migrants, and wintering species of San Diego County. The camping area survived the Cedar Fire of 2003 and still has large pines, white fir, and incense cedars. This spot is especially good for woodpeckers in the winter, where you can find six species on a good day. It's possible to find Hairy, Acorn, and Nuttall's Woodpeckers, Northern Flicker, and Williamson's, Red-naped, and Red-breasted Sapsuckers. In the past, White-headed Woodpecker was also regular at this location.

White-headed Woodpecker

70

4) Stonewall Mine

On the access drive leading to the parking lot look for Wild Turkey, Western Meadowlark, Western Bluebird, and, depending on the season, a variety of sparrows. The wooded area surrounding the parking area is good for the typical montane forest species, including White-breasted and Pygmy Nuthatches, Mountain Chickadee, and Western Wood-Pewee. This is an excellent spot for migrants, such as Cassin's Vireo, and both Townsend's and Hermit Warblers. Winter brings finches and sapsuckers. One of the trails makes a loop around a hilltop and another leads west down to Lake Cuyamaca (see the next paragraph).

5) Lake Cuyamaca

The south end of this lake has a good section of marsh, and the water here is good for dabbling ducks. Western, Pied-billed, and Eared Grebes are frequent visitors here. Wood Ducks are sometimes present. Osprey is commonly spotted and winter may bring the odd Bald Eagle. A convenient spot from which to survey the lake is the Lake Cuyamaca Restaurant and convenience store. For a fee, you can bird, picnic, and fish along the lakeside at this location. This is usually a good spot for Tricolored Blackbird, and sometimes for Lawrence's Goldfinch as well.

Driving Directions to Cuyamaca Rancho State Park Locations

Drive east from San Diego on I-8 to the Descanso Exit (exit 40, Highway 79). Drive north for 4.4 miles on Highway 79 to the south boundary of the park. From there:

- **Area 1 (Green Valley Falls)** - Drive 2.5 miles north on Highway 79 from the south boundary of the park. Turn left into the hiking/camping area and pay the day use fee. Follow signs to the falls parking area.

- **Area 2 (Visitor Center and Trails)** – From **Area 1** turn left onto Highway 79 and drive north 2.1 miles to the entry road for the park headquarters. Turn right and drive to the visitor center and parking lot.

- **Area 3 (Paso Picacho Campground)** - From **Area 2** turn right onto Highway 79 and drive 3.0 miles to the entry road for the day use area and campground. Park in this day-use parking lot and walk uphill on one of the trails, or along the road, into the forested camping area.

- **Area 4 (Stonewall Mine)** - From **Area 3** turn left onto Highway 79 and drive 0.9 miles to the entry road for this area. Turn right and

71

drive northeast 1.1 miles to the end of the road, which terminates at a parking lot.

- **Area 5 (Lake Cuyamaca)** - From **Area 4** turn right onto Highway 79 and drive 1.3 miles to the Lake Cuyamaca Restaurant and Store.

Site Notes

Best Times to Visit
- Winter is the best time to search for woodpeckers and sapsuckers
- Spring is the time to listen and look for Mountain Quail, migrants, and singing residents

Ownership: State of California

Vehicle Access: Paved roads

Fees
- Day use fees are $8 per vehicle
- Camping fees are $30 per night

Hours: Dawn until dusk

Camping
- Green Valley Campground
- Paso Picacho Campground

Restrooms: Throughout the park

Food
- Lake Cuyamaca Restaurant and convenience store (north of the park)
- Descanso (south of the park)
- Julian (8.7 miles north of Lake Cuyamaca Restaurant)

Gas
- Descanso (3.1 miles south of the southern boundary)
- Julian (8.7 miles north of Lake Cuyamaca Restaurant)

Address
Cuyamaca Rancho State Park
13652 Highway 79
Julian, CA 92036

Phone number: (760) 765-0755

Website: http://www.parks.ca.gov/?page_id=667

Mountain Warblers of
San Diego County and State Parks

Hermit – uncommon migrant that favors spruce and firs

Townsend's – common migrant in pines and other trees

Black-throated Gray – common migrant and breeder, favors oaks

Wilson's – most often seen in riparian areas, but may be found anywhere – the most common of our migrant warblers

MacGillivray's – a fairly common but retiring migrant warbler of thick brushy areas

Common Yellowthroat – common breeder in wet areas, like the marshes and brush around Lake Cuyamaca

Yellow – common breeder in riparian areas

Yellow-rumped – common winter visitor and migrant in wooded areas and urban neighborhoods

Nashville – common migrant in riparian areas

Orange-crowned – common migrant and less common winter visitor in riparian areas

L. Mission Trails Regional Park

Habitat
- Riparian areas with extensive, mature cottonwood and willow forest
- Lake
- Marshes
- Mesquite and desert scrub
- Desert washes
- Desert mountains and cliffs

Target Birds
- Osprey
- White-tailed Kite (occasional breeder)
- Red-shouldered Hawk (resident)
- Hummingbirds: Anna's, Allen's, Black-chinned, and Rufous (resident and migrant)
- Nuttall's Woodpecker (resident)
- Falcons: Merlin, Prairie, and Peregrine (winter)
- Greater Roadrunner (resident)
- Loggerhead Shrike (winter)
- California Thrasher (resident)
- California Gnatcatcher (resident)
- Wrens: House, Rock, Canyon, and Bewick's (resident)
- Wrentit (resident)
- Phainopepla (summer)
- Western warblers and flycatchers (migration)
- Blue Grosbeak (summer)
- California Towhee (resident)
- Sparrows: Rufous-crowned (resident), White-crowned (winter), Fox (winter), and Grasshopper (summer)
- Towhees: Spotted (resident), Green-tailed (winter), and California (resident)

General Description
This 6800-acre park has almost sixty miles of trails which wind through mountains, chaparral, riparian woodlands along the San Diego River, two small lakes, and the historic Mission Dam. It is only twelve miles from downtown San Diego. Many of the trails are very scenic and take you to a wide variety of habitats. Look here for common chaparral and foothills

species like Western Scrub-Jay, wrens, thrashers, towhees, goldfinches, and orioles. The riparian areas hold flycatchers, Bell's Vireo, Yellow-breasted Chat, buntings, and Yellow Warbler. This park can be quite crowded on weekends, and parking your vehicle may be a challenge—so the best advice is to come early on a weekday, when the crowds are much thinner and the birds are easier to both see and hear.

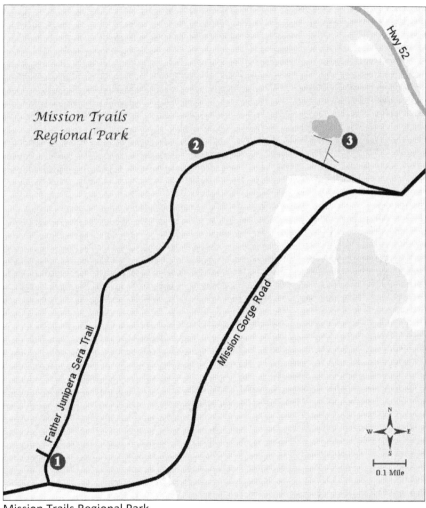

Mission Trails Regional Park

Birding Suggestions

1) Visitor Center and Oak Grove Trail

The headquarters has brochures and birding information and is open from 8:00 a.m. - 4:30 p.m. Monday through Friday. If you

Bewick's Wren

get to the location before the parking lot is open, you can park in the small lot for the Oak Grove Trail, or along the road. The Oak Grove Trail is a short loop trail across the road from the visitor center that provides a nice introduction to the birds of the park. Look for Anna's, Allen's, and Rufous Hummingbirds at flowering shrubs in the late summer. Wrentit, California Gnatcatcher, Lesser Goldfinch, California Thrasher, and California Towhee all breed here. Other small passerines to look for include Hutton's Vireo, and both House and Bewick's Wrens.

2) Old Mission Dam and Oak Canyon

A scenic trail skirts the 18th century dam and ponds, borders brushy mountainsides, and then follows the San Diego River through fine riparian areas. Listen and look for Red-shouldered Hawk. Pacific-slope and Ash-throated Flycatchers are here in the summer and Black Phoebes year round. Bushtit and up to four species of wrens are common, as are hummingbirds. Migration brings all kinds of western flycatchers and warblers to the area. Look for resident Song Sparrow in the riparian areas and resident Rufous-crowned Sparrow and California Towhee on the hillsides.

3) Kumeyaay Lake and Campground

Search along the trails for breeding Nuttall's Woodpecker, Ash-throated Flycatcher, Bushtit, Western Bluebird, Bell's Vireo, and Lesser Goldfinch. Less common, but also breeding, are Cooper's Hawk, Phainopepla, and Blue Grosbeak. A variety of common waterfowl (Northern Pintail, Cinnamon Teal, and Ruddy Duck) visit the small lake in the winter. The lake is surrounded by cattails, which hide Common Yellowthroat, Song Sparrow, and Common Gallinule.

Least Bittern may also be there. In the spring and early summer listen for the insect-like trill of the Grasshopper Sparrow in the verdant fields around the camping area.

Driving Directions to Park Locations

This large park is twelve miles northeast of San Diego, several miles north of Interstate 8 and immediately south of Highway 52. The directions here all start in the center of Santee, the closest city, which is immediately east of the park.

- **Area 1 (Visitor Center)** – You'll need to access the visitor center from the south entrance of the park at Mission Gorge Road, since Father Junipero Serro Trail is a one-way road until you reach the Mission Dam parking lot.
  - From the center of Santee take Mission Gorge Road 5.6 miles south to reach Father Junipero Serra Trail.
  - Turn right onto Father Junipero Serra Trail and drive north 0.1 mile to the visitor center entry road. Park along the road or in the small lot for the Oak Grove Trail if the visitor center lot is not yet open.
- **Area 2 (Mission Dam)** - From the visitor center turn left back onto Father Junipero Serra Trail and drive 1.8 miles to the Mission Dam parking lot turn-off. There is a small parking lot here, which fills up quickly during peak visiting times.
- **Area 3 (Lake and Campgrounds)** – From the Mission Dam parking lot turn left on Father Junipero Serra Trail and drive 0.5 miles to the campground entrance on the left. You can park in the day-use parking area for free and then walk down to the lake.

Site Notes

Best Time to Visit: Spring has pleasant temperatures and the best chance for both migrants and breeding birds – and the birds will be singing

Ownership: City of San Diego

Vehicle Access: Paved roads are fine for 2-wheel drive

Fees: No day-use fee; $22 per night for camping

Hours: Visitor center open daily 9:00 a.m. – 5:00 p.m.

Camping: Kumeyaay Lake Campground

Restrooms: Visitor center, campground, and at some of the trailheads

Food: The city of Santee, to the east, has lots of choices

Gas: Santee

Address
Mission Trails Regional Park and Visitor Center
One Father Junipero Serra Tr.
San Diego, CA 92119
Phone: (619) 668-3281
Website: http://www.mtrp.org/

M. Lindo Lake County Park

Habitat
- Oak, pine, and eucalyptus parklands
- Lake
- Wetlands and marsh

Target Birds
- Geese: Ross's, Snow, Greater White-fronted, and Canada (resident and wintering)
- Ducks: Wood (resident), three species of teal (winter), and dabbling ducks (winter)
- Black-crowned Night-Heron (resident)
- Red-shouldered Hawk (resident)
- Woodpeckers: Acorn and Nuttall's (resident)
- Red-breasted Sapsucker (winter)
- Oak Titmouse (resident)
- Western warblers (mostly migration)
- Lawrence's Goldfinch (irruptive)
- Tricolored Blackbird (sometimes breeds)
- Hooded Oriole (summer)

General Description
This small park is within the city limits of Lakeside. In addition to recreational activities such as picnicking, fishing, baseball, tennis, skateboarding, and a playground, there are good opportunities for birding here. During the winter season a number of waterfowl join the resident geese and Wood Ducks. The close proximity to so many benign park-goers (and the occasional feeding) makes some of them quite tame, and excellent photographic subjects. The same goes for the resident Black-crowned Night-Herons,

Wood Duck

which often stand around waiting for fishermen to toss them a morsel. During winter be on the lookout for sapsuckers, nuthatches, kinglets, and chickadees which come down from the nearby mountains. Some years are good for Tricolored Blackbirds.

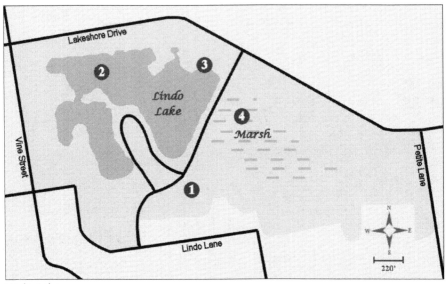

Lindo Lake

Birding Suggestions

1) Woodlands

The many trees in this park are a good place to find Acorn and Nuttall's Woodpeckers, Oak Titmouse, and White-breasted Nuthatch. Red-shouldered Hawk is often heard and usually seen. The residents are joined by finches and other montane forest birds during some winters. Cedar Waxwing and sapsuckers are regular winter visitors.

2) Lindo Lake

This park is a reliable spot to see one of our most beautiful species of waterfowl, the Wood Duck. As in many parks, Canada Geese have staked out their claim. In winter these breeders are joined by many dabblers, a few diving ducks, and other geese. White-fronted and Ross's Geese may remain well into the summer, and some years they even take up residence. Other birds that enjoy these waters are Eared Grebe, American White Pelican, Double-crested Cormorant, Caspian and Forster's Terns, and Bonaparte's Gulls.

80

3) Cattail Stand

The cattails are home to Red-winged and, sometimes, Tricolored Blackbirds. Marsh Wren and Song Sparrow are resident, and joined by Lincoln's Sparrow in the winter. Sora and Virginia Rail may also be here in the winter, and Common Gallinule is resident. At times Vermilion Flycatcher will join the much more common Black Phoebe here and around the lake.

4) Wetlands

On the east side of the causeway is a marshy area (water-filled after heavy rains) that is attractive to three species of teal, blackbirds, shorebirds, and sparrows in the winter. Look for Red-shouldered and Red-tailed Hawks perched on the trees that surround this low area. During summer this area may dry out completely.

Anna's Hummingbird

Driving Directions to Lindo Lake

- From I-8, approximately 15 miles east of San Diego
  - Merge onto CA-67 north and drive north for 5.0 miles to the Winter Gardens exit.
  - Take the exit and drive south on Winter Gardens Blvd. for 0.3 miles to Woodside Avenue.
  - Turn left onto Woodside Avenue; Woodside Avenue becomes Chestnut Street; Chestnut Street becomes Lindo Lane.
  - After 0.8 miles turn left into the park.
- Park close to site 2 (downhill from the restrooms) and you'll be able to walk to each of the locations detailed above.

Site Notes

Best Time to Visit: Winter has the most birds: waterfowl, waders, raptors, and wintering passerines

Ownership: San Diego County

Vehicle Access: Paved roads

Fees: None

Hours: Open from 9:30 a.m. to sunset

Restrooms: In the park

Food: Lakeside

Gas: Lakeside

Address

Lindo Lake County Park

12660 Lindo Lane

Lakeside, CA 92040

Phone number: (619) 443-1666

Website: http://www.sandiegocounty.gov/parks/picnic/lindolake.html

N. Pine Valley

Habitat
- Residential areas and city parks
- Streams and meadows
- Riparian areas
- Chaparral
- Pine and oak woodlots

Target Birds
- California Quail (resident)
- Red-shouldered Hawk (resident)
- Woodpeckers: Acorn and Nuttall's (resident)
- Phoebes: Black and Say's (resident)
- Loggerhead Shrike (winter)
- Jays: Steller's and Western Scrub-Jay (resident)
- Western swallows (migration and resident)
- Oak Titmouse (resident)
- Nuthatches: Pygmy and White-breasted (resident)
- Western Bluebird (resident)
- California Thrasher (resident)
- Western warblers (mostly migrants)
- Towhees: Spotted and California (resident), Green-tailed (winter)
- Sparrows: Chipping, Lark, White-crowned and Golden-crowned (winter)
- Lazuli Bunting: (migration and summer)

General Description
This small town of 1500 residents is nestled at the base of the Laguna Mountain Recreation Area. The town is nicely wooded and several residents feed birds year round; even more residents put out feed in the winter. At these feeding stations during the winter months keep an eye out for Acorn, Nuttall's, and Hairy Woodpeckers, hummingbirds, jays, Mountain Chickadee, Oak Titmouse, White-breasted Nuthatch, Pine Siskin, Cassin's Finch, Spotted Towhee, and sparrows.

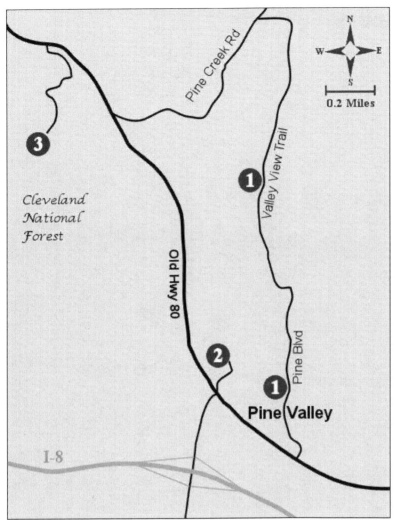

Pine Valley

Birding Suggestions for Pine Valley

1) Pine Boulevard and Valley View Trail

During the 2015 winter season Pine Boulevard and Valley View Trail were good roads to drive or walk along to view several active bird-feeding stations. Parking along this road may be difficult in some areas, but you can park more easily on some of the side streets. In addition to many of the resident mountain birds, look during the winter for Pine Siskin, Cassin's Finch, Red Crossbill, Golden-crowned Sparrow, and Chipping Sparrow.

2) Pine Valley County Park

This park has ball fields, a basketball court, picnic areas, and tennis courts. Search the small wooded areas for woodpeckers, sapsuckers, flycatchers, and warblers. The meadows and brushy fringes of the park hide sparrows and towhees.

3) Pine Creek Trail/Secret Canyon

This scenic area is just northwest of the city; it is the beginning of a long, 15.6-mile, stream-side trail going through the Pine Creek Wilderness. Among the many birds, look for Lazuli Bunting in the spring and early summer, and woodpeckers, jays, vireos, California Thrasher, warblers, and sparrows year round.

Driving Directions to Pine Valley Locations

- **Area 1 (Pine Blvd.)** – From I-8 take exit 45 for Pine Valley and drive north 0.4 miles to Old Highway 80. Turn right on Old Highway 80 and drive 0.4 miles to Laguna Trail. Turn left on Laguna Trail and drive one block north to Pine Blvd. Turn left onto Pine Blvd. to enter the residential area. Drive or walk along Pine Blvd. and Valley View Trail for 1.9 miles, looking at the feeders along the way.

- **Area 2 (Pine Valley County Park)** – From I-8 take exit 45 for Pine Valley and drive north 0.4 miles to Old Highway 80. Cross Highway 80 to the park entrance on the north side of the road.

- **Area 3 (Pine Creek)** – From I-8 take exit 45 for Pine Valley and drive north 0.4 miles to Old Highway 80. Turn left on Old Highway 80 and drive 1.6 miles to the Pine Creek Trailhead turn-off (just past milepost 3.5). Turn left onto the entrance road and follow it 0.4 miles to the parking area; take the trail leading downstream to the southwest or walk along the old fire road to bird the area.

Site Notes

Ownership
- Private yards
- San Diego County
- Cleveland National Forest

Vehicle Access: All roads are accessible by automobile

Fees: If visiting Pine Creek Trail, you'll need either a Forest Adventure Pass or a National Parks Annual Pass

Hours: Pine Valley County Park is open from 9:30 a.m. to ½ hour before sunset

Restrooms
- Restaurants/gas station in Pine Valley
- Pine Valley County Park
- Pit toilet at Pine Creek trailhead

Food: Restaurant and groceries in Pine Valley

Gas: One station in Pine Valley, but gas is less expensive 15 miles to the east, off of I-8, at the Golden Acorn Casino

Address
Pine Valley County Park
28810 Old Highway 80
Pine Valley, CA 91962

Phone: Pine Valley County Park: (619) 473-8558

Website: http://www.sandiegocounty.gov/parks/picnic/pinevalley.html

American Kestrel

O. Laguna Mountain Recreation Area

Habitat
- Mixed oak and pine forest
- Meadows
- Streams
- Seasonal ponds
- Chaparral
- Desert mountains

Target Birds
- Red-shouldered Hawk (resident)
- Golden Eagle (rare resident)
- Quail: Mountain and California (resident)
- Owls: Western Screech-Owl, Northern Saw-whet, and Spotted (resident)
- Woodpeckers: Hairy, Acorn and Nuttall's (resident)
- Sapsuckers: Red-naped, Red-breasted, and Williamson's (winter)
- Loggerhead Shrike (winter)
- Violet-green Swallow (summer)
- Jays: Steller's and Western Scrub-Jay (resident)
- Nuthatches: Pygmy and White-breasted (resident)
- Mountain Chickadee (resident)
- Oak Titmouse (resident)
- Western Bluebird (resident)
- California Thrasher (resident)
- Phainopepla (spring)
- Western warblers (mostly migration)
- Towhees: Spotted and California (resident)
- Sparrows: Lark, Chipping, Fox, and White-crowned (resident and winter)
- Brewer's Blackbird
- Finches: Cassin's and Purple (irruptive)
- Goldfinches: Lesser (resident) and Lawrence's (irruptive)

General Description
This is a well-forested area, having mostly escaped the ravages of the 2003 Cedar Fire. Lower areas have nice stands of live oak; higher areas are mostly pine. There are large areas of chaparral and shrub on the

edges of the forest and in the areas that were burned. There are outstanding views of the desert mountains and canyons to the east; these are part of Anza Borrego Desert State Park. Over 70 miles of trails provide access to the various habitats. Just about every montane bird seen in San Diego County has visited this area at one time or another, and many are resident. Some years bring an influx of sapsuckers, Cassin's and Purple Finches, Red Crossbill, Pinyon Jay (rare), and Clark's Nutcracker (rare). More commonly seen, though, are Nuttall's and Acorn Woodpeckers, Northern Flicker, Oak Titmouse, Mountain Chickadee, Hermit Thrush, Pine Siskin, Steller's Jay, Pygmy and White-breasted Nuthatches, and both Spotted and Green-tailed (winter) Towhees. Watch the skies for accipiters and the occasional Golden Eagle. Owling in this area can be productive in the spring for Spotted Owl and Northern Saw-whet Owl.

Spotted Towhee

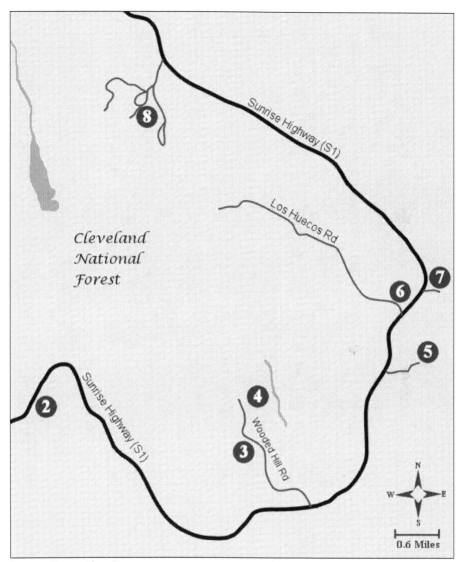

Laguna Recreation Area

Birding Suggestions

1) Sunrise Highway Overlook
(Not shown on the map above, it's 3.9 miles downhill from site 2)
From I-8, take Sunrise Highway (S1) for 1.7 miles uphill to the second overlook. This area of dense chaparral has resident Spotted Towhee, California Thrasher, Blue-gray Gnatcatcher, and Wrentit. A

trail leads down the mountain and into the chaparral—this will take you to areas farther from the highway where you'll have better chances to hear and see summering Black-chinned Sparrow and Gray Vireo (but both these species are much easier to find above Buckman Springs Rest Area).

2) Laguna Mountain Recreation Area

This Cleveland National Forest recreation area covers 8000 acres and offers many opportunities for birding, hiking, and camping. The parking area here at the boundary of the recreation area is the starting point for several trails which have yielded Clark's Nutcracker and Pinyon Jay in the winter during the past few years. It's also a very popular spot for San Diegan lowlanders to visit during the rare (but regular) snowy weekends.

Northern Saw-whet Owl

3) Wooded Hill Trail

This half-mile trail starts at the base of Wooded Hill and circles the hill before returning to the parking area. There's a fine view from the top of the hill. Violet-green Swallow breeds in the trees and can be seen from late spring through the summer months. This is also a good early-spring spot to hunt for the elusive and often quite wary Mountain Quail—listen for their distinctive "Quark" call drifting from the forest. As you walk this pleasant trail you'll encounter many of the common pine-oaks woodland birds that call these mountains home.

4) Agua Dulce Spring and Stream

With a constant source of water, this is one of the most consistently good birding areas in the Laguna Mountains. Many birds fly down to drink here from the surrounding hills, and by watching from a seat on the hillside overlooking the stream crossing you'll be able to see a great variety of species. We have gotten Mountain Quail on almost every visit, either heard or seen. One or two Nuttall's Woodpeckers always seem to be in the area, along with dozens of Acorn Woodpeckers. Warblers and sparrows like to come in and drink from beneath the thick underbrush lining the stream, and Hermit Thrush is often found. Flycatchers, Cassin's Vireo, and migrant warblers pick off the insects drawn to the area. And lastly, keep a look out for the resident Red-shouldered Hawk.

Hermit Thrush

5) Burnt Rancheria Campground

This large campground has a nice nature trail in the middle of it. At the extreme northeastern corner, overlooking the Anza Borrego Desert, is a concrete wildlife watering trough. Especially in the summer, the water is a magnet for birds, and you can get excellent close-up photos of nuthatches, titmice, chickadees, bluebirds, and other passerines as they come in to drink. The campground is at 6000 ft and closes in the winter (end of October-April), but by walking in from the gate you can still look for cold-weather, bird-feeding flocks.

6) Visitor Center

A short trail behind this visitor center parking lot provides access to some of the forest habitats, but more interesting and productive (at least in the winter) are the bird feeders. You'll have an opportunity to get close views of Pine Siskin, Oak Titmouse, Mountain Chickadee, and both Pygmy and White-breasted Nuthatch. During migration look for Townsend's, Nashville, Yellow, and other warblers as they feed in the oaks and evergreens surrounding the small visitor center. Inside, you'll find maps and other publications for sale, and the staff can provide information about forest trails.

7) Desert View Picnic Area

A nice trail that starts here travels south along the ridgeline overlooking the desert mountains of Anza Borrego Desert State Park. The trail goes through stands of short, red-barked manzanita trees and other shrubs; watch for resident Fox Sparrow, California Thrasher, and Spotted Towhees. As you look out over the peaks and badlands, you may spot soaring Common Raven, Red-tailed Hawk, and Golden Eagle. If you hike the trail south along the ridge long enough (approximately 1.5 miles) you'll reach the Burnt Rancheria Campgrounds, and the productive wildlife watering trough.

8) Laguna Campground Area

This large camping area has mature pines, some fine meadows, and ephemeral ponds. Chipping Sparrow is a common resident, as are White-breasted and Pygmy Nuthatches, Mountain Chickadee, Western Bluebird, and occasionally Western Meadowlark. Red-tailed Hawk and American Kestrel patrol the meadows and forest edges. There are many trails in the area. One trail connects to Wooded Hill (**Area 3**) and another to the parking area at the start of the Laguna Recreation Area (**Area 2**). Exploring these trails may turn up some of the more rare birds for this area, like Pinyon Jay and Clark's Nutcracker.

Mountain Chickadee

The Warblers of San Diego County Mountain Parks

Hermit – uncommon migrant that favors spruce and firs

Townsend's – common migrant in pines

Black-throated Gray – common migrant and breeder, favors oaks

Wilson's – most often seen in riparian areas, but may be found anywhere – the most common of our migrants

MacGillivray's – a fairly common but retiring warbler of thick brushy areas

Common Yellowthroat – common breeder in wet areas, like the marshes and brush around Lake Cuyamaca

Yellow – common breeder in riparian areas

Yellow-rumped – common winter visitor and migrant in many wooded areas and urban neighborhoods

Nashville – common migrant in riparian areas

Orange-crowned – common migrant and less common winter visitor in riparian areas

Driving Directions for Laguna Mountain Recreation Area

Except for Area 4, the beginning spot for these locations is the intersection of I-8 and Sunrise Highway.

- **Area 1 (Sunrise Highway Overlook)** – Drive uphill 1.7 miles; the overlook is on the right (east) side of the road.
- **Area 2 (Laguna Mountain Recreation Area)** – Drive uphill 5.6 miles; parking is on both sides of the road and the trails are on the left.
- **Area 3 (Wooded Hill Trail)** – The turn-off to this area is 8.2 miles uphill; the parking lot for Wooded Hill Trail is 0.3 miles up the access road.
- **Area 4 (Agua Dulce Spring and Stream)** – From the Wooded Hill Trail parking lot (**Area 3**) drive north 0.3 miles into the Agua Dulce Camping Area (just a small round-about). Take the trail downhill and northeast; take the first left; another left; you'll soon be heading northwest along the creek. Keep going toward the pump house and Agua Dulce Creek crossing (GPS coordinates are 32.856907, -116.433294).

- **Area 5 (Burnt Rancheria Campground)** – Drive uphill 9.4 miles; the campground is on the right (east) side of the road.
- **Area 6 (Visitor Center)** – Drive uphill 9.9 miles; the visitor center and parking lot are on the left (west) side of Sunrise Highway.
- **Area 7 (Desert View Picnic Area)** – Drive uphill 10.2 miles; the picnic area is on the right (east) side of the road.
- **Area 8 (Laguna Campground)** – Drive uphill 12.7 miles; the turnoff to this large area is on the left side of the road.

Site Notes

Ownership
- Cleveland National Forest
- Private

Vehicle Access
- The main roads going through the forest are either paved or are high-quality gravel and accessible by automobile.
- A few of the secondary roads leading downhill away from the recreation area require high clearance, especially after storms or winter snows. Most of these secondary roads are closed during the winter.

Fees
- Either a Forest Adventure pass ($5 for a day or $30 per year) or a National Parks Annual Pass is required to visit these sites
- Camping fees: $22 +
- Restrooms: Campgrounds, visitor center, and some picnic areas

Camping
- Reservations for many of these camping sites can be made on-line via: http://www.reserveamerica.com/unifSearchResults.do
- Wooded Hill, Burnt Rancheria, and Laguna Campgrounds ($22.00+)
- There is no primitive/undeveloped camping available in the Laguna Mountain Recreation Area

Food
- A large convenience/grocery store is situated along Sunrise Highway in the Laguna Mountain Recreation Area—you can also purchase Forest Adventure passes there
- Convenience and grocery stores in Pine Valley
- Several restaurants are along the Sunrise Highway in the Laguna Mountain Recreation Area and in Pine Valley

Gas
- One gas station at Pine Valley Store, in Pine Valley
- Less expensive gas is at Golden Acorn Casino, 14.5 miles to the east, on the south side of I-8

P. Buckman Springs Area

Habitat
- Chaparral
- Riparian
- Meadows

Target Birds
- California Quail (resident)
- Phoebes: Black and Say's (resident)
- Loggerhead Shrike (winter)
- Western Scrub-Jay (resident)
- Gray Vireo (summer)
- Canyon Wren (resident)
- Wrentit (resident)
- California Thrasher (resident)
- Spotted Towhee (resident)
- Black-chinned Sparrow (summer)
- Fox Sparrow (winter)

General Description
This pleasant valley offers birders several locations to search for chaparral, montane, and riparian species, and even a few waterfowl at Lake Morena. The Pacific Coast Trail winds along Kitchen Creek and crosses through Boulder Oaks Campground. Sheephead Mountain Road provides access to good chaparral with breeding Gray Vireo and Black-chinned Sparrow, one of the easier spots to search for these species in the county. The road continues up the mountain to a favorite take-off point for hang gliders. At times the winds in this valley are truly ferocious, even blowing over tractor trailers. Of course, birding becomes more challenging then.

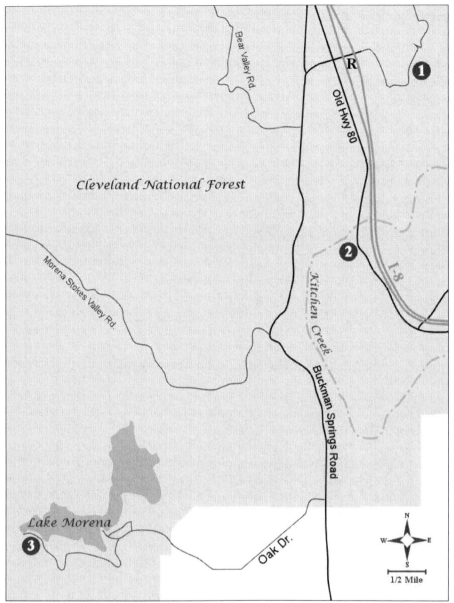

Buckman Springs and Lake Morena, **R** – Rest Area

Birding Suggestions

1) Sheephead Mountain Road

Gray Vireo

This is an excellent location to find common chaparral species in addition to some less common ones. Drive up the hillside to a pullout about a quarter of a mile and park. In the spring and early summer the drainage and surrounding bushes are a reliable spot to listen and look for both Gray Vireo and Black-chinned Sparrow. Other species here include Western Scrub-Jay, California Thrasher, Spotted Towhee, and Wrentit. From time to time we have also heard Canyon Wren here.

2) Boulder Oaks Campground

This pleasant park is a good place to look for chaparral birds down at eye level, as well as migrants and wintering birds. Fox Sparrows, especially, like the brush here. Despite the name, there aren't many oaks. However, it's easy to bird along the road just south of the park and find Nuttall's Woodpecker, Oak Titmouse, and Western Bluebird.

3) Lake Morena County Park

In winter, stop along the shore and scope the lake for waterfowl. Too many years of drought have reduced the once sizeable lake to a fraction of its original size—hopefully future rains will restore it to its former self. Green Heron is resident, and Belted Kingfisher joins it during the winter. At the south end of the park is a short interpretive trail that passes through chaparral and mixed woods. Look here for Wrentit, Western Scrub-Jay, towhees, goldfinches, and seasonal migrants.

> ### *Birds of the Mountain Chaparral*
>
> **Mountain Quail** – common but retiring resident; best time to spot one is when they are calling and displaying in the spring
>
> **California Quail** – common resident, but may be difficult to see in the brushy chaparral
>
> **Wrentit** – common resident, but much more often heard than seen
>
> **California Thrasher** – common resident, this bird is often spotted singing from a perch in the spring or summer
>
> **Blue-gray Gnatcatcher** – common wintering visitor
>
> **Western Scrub-Jay** – common and noisy resident; usually responds well to squeaking and pishing
>
> **Gray Vireo** – uncommon and retiring breeder, best chance is during the spring when they are singing
>
> **California Towhee** – common to abundant resident, but may be hard to spot in the brush; chaparral with lots of open areas like Cabrillo National Monument makes seeing them a breeze
>
> **Spotted Towhee** – very common resident; they call often, and will usually perch up if you're patient
>
> **Fox Sparrow** – common migrant and winter visitor
>
> **Black-chinned Sparrow** – uncommon in many areas; listen for distinctive song; try the hills north of the Kitchen Creek Campground or Buckman Springs

Driving Directions for Buckman Springs Locations

- **Area 1 (Sheephead Mountain Road)** – Take exit 51 from Interstate 8. Turn east onto Sheephead Mountain Road and follow the gravel/dirt road for 0.5 miles as it turns toward the south. Follow the same road as it turns west and north, and heads up the mountainside. Check the shrubby drainage at 0.3 miles for vireos and sparrows. (This gravel road does have some ruts, so if you're in a ground-hugging car, you should walk this stretch.)
- **Area 2 (Boulder Oaks Campground)** –Take exit 51 from Interstate 8. Drive several hundred feet west to Old Highway 80. Drive south 2.2 miles on Old Highway 80 to the Boulder Oaks Campground, which will be on your right (west side).

- **Area 3 (Lake Morena County Park)** – Take exit 51 from Interstate 8. Drive 5.4 miles west and south on Buckman Springs Road. Turn right onto Oak Drive and drive 2.3 miles to the entrance of the park.

Site Notes

Ownership
- Bureau of Land Management
- Cleveland National Forest
- County of San Diego
- Private

Vehicle Access
- Paved roads provide access to Sites 1-3. Sheephead Mountain Road, which goes up the side of the hill to the vireos and sparrows, is best done with a high-clearance vehicle. However, it's easy to drive and park at the base of the hill with a car and then hike a third of a mile up to the good spots.

Fees: Fee required to visit or camp at Lake Morena County Park

Hours: Lake Morena County Park is open from sunrise to sunset

Restrooms
- Buckman Springs Rest Area
- Lake Morena County Park
- Boulder Oaks Campground

Camping
- Primitive (free) camping on BLM and forest lands surrounding the area
- Boulder Oaks ($12+), call 619-445-6235 to inquire about the availability of water
- Lake Morena County Park ($22+)

Food
- Golden Acorn Casino convenience store is 10.6 miles east
- Restaurant at Pine Valley is 5.6 miles west

Gas: Golden Acorn Casino is 10.6 miles east

Q. Kitchen Creek Road and Cibbets Flat Campground

Habitat
- Oak and pine woodlands
- Riparian areas along Kitchen Creek
- Mountain chaparral

Target Birds
- Mountain Quail (resident)
- Hawks: Red-shouldered and Red-tailed (resident)
- Anna's Hummingbird (resident)
- Woodpeckers: Acorn and Nuttall's (resident)
- Steller's Jay (resident)
- Western Scrub-Jay (resident)
- Oak Titmouse (resident)
- Wrens: Bewick's and Rock (resident)
- Western warblers (mostly migration)
- Towhees: Spotted and California (resident)
- Black-chinned Sparrow (summer)
- Lazuli Bunting (summer)
- Scott's Oriole (summer)
- Lawrence's Goldfinch (usually summer, occasionally in winter)

General Description
Especially if driving into San Diego County from the east, this site is a great introduction to the birds of the Laguna Mountains. But even if you're arriving from the west, it's still a fine spot to look for some of the specialty birds of the area, such as Mountain Quail, Black-chinned Sparrow, and Lawrence's Goldfinch. A nice campground is situated at the end of Kitchen Creek Road, which is a good place to find some of the common birds of the Laguna Mountains, such as Acorn Woodpecker, Western Bluebird, White-breasted Nuthatch, and both Steller's Jay and Western Scrub-Jay.

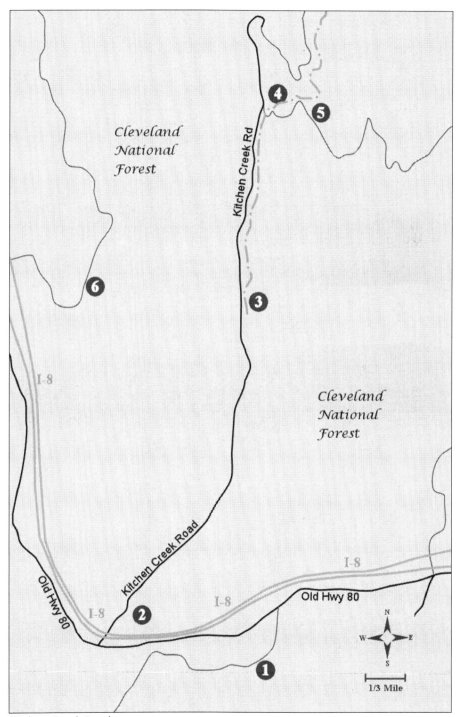

Kitchen Creek Road

Birding Suggestions

1) Cameron Truck Trail

Check the sage-covered hill south of the Border Patrol Station for Bell's Sparrow, especially in the spring. Other sparrows, such as Lark, Brewer's, and Chipping may be present in winter. Ash-throated Flycatcher is common in the summer and Say's Phoebe is common in the winter. The surrounding hillsides have a typical assortment of chaparral birds.

2) Fire Station

The scattered brush, grasslands, and mature trees around this fire station are good for Western Kingbird, Say's Phoebe, Western Bluebird, Black-headed Grosbeak, Chipping and Lark Sparrows, and in migration, several oriole species. When birding this area, please don't block any of the roads.

3) Yellow Rose Spring

One late spring afternoon we heard Mountain Quail calling on the west hillside (to the left of the road as you're heading north up to Cibbets Flat). After some searching we finally saw a male calling from the top of a boulder close to the crest and were able to watch it well through the scope. In the sycamores and live oaks on the east side of the road look for Acorn and Nuttall's Woodpeckers, Phainopepla, and both Lesser and Lawrence's Goldfinches, all of which breed here. Other birds that frequent this verdant valley include Wrentit, California Towhee, Spotted Towhee, California

Lawrence's Goldfinches

Thrasher, and three species of orioles. Watch the skies above for resident Red-tailed Hawk and Golden Eagle.

4) and 5) Cibbets Flat Campground and Fred Canyon Road

Western Bluebird

Kitchen Creek runs beside this campground and along with the conifers, oaks, and brush provides an excellent home for birds. Look for Acorn and Nuttall's Woodpeckers, Bushtit, Western Bluebird, Western Scrub-Jay, Bewick's Wren, Oak Titmouse, California Towhee, Lazuli Bunting, and Lesser Goldfinch. Winter brings Steller's Jay, Hermit Thrush, Spotted Towhee, American Robin, and Mountain Chickadee. During some winters the campground host's feeding station brings in Mountain Quail. The surrounding hillsides feature a good chaparral community, and harbor breeding Mountain Quail, Western Scrub-Jay, California Thrasher, and Black-chinned Sparrow. The bouncing-ball song of the Black-chinned Sparrow is easily heard on spring mornings in late April and early May as you walk up Fred Canyon Road (gravel and dirt) that skirts the campground and heads uphill. During spring and fall expect good numbers of western migrants. A morning spring walk along the Kitchen Creek trail may reward you with Western Wood-Pewee, Hammond's Flycatcher, Cassin's and Hutton's Vireos, Wilson's and Townsend's Warblers, Lazuli Bunting, and both Black-headed and Blue Grosbeaks.

6) Buckman Springs
Please see previous chapter for a description of this location.

> ## The Warblers of San Diego County Mountain Parks
>
> **Hermit** – uncommon migrant that favors spruce and firs
> **Townsend's** – common migrant in pines
> **Black-throated Gray** – common migrant and breeder, favors oaks
> **Wilson's** – most often seen in riparian areas, but may be found anywhere – the most common of our migrants
> **MacGillivray's** – a fairly common but retiring warbler of thick brushy areas
> **Common Yellowthroat** – common breeder in wet areas, like the marshes and brush around Lake Cuyamaca
> **Yellow** – common breeder in riparian areas
> **Yellow-rumped** – common winter visitor and migrant in many wooded areas and urban neighborhoods
> **Nashville** – common migrant in riparian areas
> **Orange-crowned** – common migrant and less common winter visitor in riparian areas

Driving Directions to Kitchen Creek Road Birding Locations

- **Area 1 (Cameron Truck Trail)** – From exit 54 on I-8, head south and then east on Old Highway 80 for 1.6 miles to Cameron Truck Trail (just past the U.S. Border Patrol complex). Turn right on Cameron Truck Trail and drive 0.3 miles to the sagebrush flats behind the station.

- **Area 2 (Fire Station)** – From exit 54 on I-8, head north 0.3 miles to the fire station turn-off. Turn right into the fire station complex. Please do not park in such a way that you are blocking any roads.

- **Area 3 (Yellow Rose Spring)** – Yellow Rose Spring and the small grove of live oaks is 2.9 miles north of I-8 on Kitchen Creek Road.

- **Area 4 (Cibbets Flat Campground)** – The turnoff to Cibbets Flat Campground is 4.7 miles north of I-8. Turn right and drive 0.2 miles over the Kitchen Creek ford to the campground turnoff. Turn left into the campground. If you have a high-clearance vehicle you can drive past the campground entrance up Ford Canyon Road for 0.5

miles to access the creek trail (and avoid the campground day-use fee).

- **Area 5 (Fred Canyon Road)** – If you have a high-clearance vehicle you can drive past the Cibbets Flat Campground entrance and go up Fred Canyon Road for 0.5 miles to access the creek trail (and avoid the campground day-use fee).

Site Notes

Best Time to Visit: Late April through early May is the best time for singing residents and the most migrants

Ownership: Cleveland National Forest

Vehicle Access: Paved and gravel roads; to go north of Cibbets Flat Campground on the gravel track you'll need a high-clearance vehicle

Fees: Camping and day-use fee at Cibbets Flat Campground

Restrooms
- Cibbets Flat Campground
- Golden Acorn gas station

Food: Live Oak Springs and Golden Acorn Casino convenience store

Gas: Live Oak Springs and Golden Acorn Casino gas stations

R. Jacumba Hot Springs

Habitat
- Urban neighborhood
- Riparian woods
- Pond and cattail marsh
- Mesquites and desert scrub
- Planted and fallow agricultural lands

Target Birds
- California Quail (resident)
- Barn Owl (resident)
- Greater Roadrunner (resident)
- Red-naped Sapsucker (winter)
- Loggerhead Shrike (resident)
- Western Scrub-Jay (resident)
- Wrens: Bewick's (resident) and House (winter)
- California Thrasher (resident)
- Phainopepla (resident)
- Warblers: numerous migrants
- Sparrows: Bell's, Brewer's, Lark, Lincoln's, and White-crowned (resident and winter)
- Tricolored Blackbird (resident, but easiest when breeding)
- Orioles: Scott's, Hooded, and Bullock's (summer, rarely in winter)
- Lawrence's Goldfinch (resident)

General Description
This small town lies on the eastern slope of the Laguna Mountains at an altitude of 2800 ft. It is a remarkably birdy location, and boasts a more diverse and wider array of species than you might expect. Here you'll find a pond with a cattail marsh surrounded by cottonwoods and other trees, green neighborhoods, agricultural areas, and surrounding desert with scrub and chaparral. During winter months look for montane species, which visit the yards and feeders. Rarities seem to visit every season, and have included Harris's Hawk, Swamp Sparrow, and Baltimore Oriole. Birds to look for in this area include California Quail, California Thrasher, Western Scrub-Jay, Tricolored Blackbird, Scott's and Hooded Orioles, Canyon and Spotted Towhees, and Lesser and Lawrence's Goldfinches.

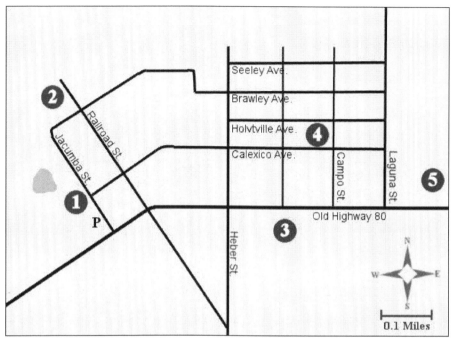

Jacumba Hot Springs, P - Parking

Birding Suggestions

1) Riparian Area and Cattail Pond

At the northwest corner of Old Highway 80 and Jacumba Street is the abandoned shell of a former spa. Park here and check the palm trees and cottonwoods for Barn Owl and Hooded Oriole. Behind this spot are two shallow ponds with seasonal Sora, Virginia Rail, and Wilson's Snipe. The big cottonwoods are also good for Oak Titmouse and migrants. In winter look for sapsuckers, waxwings, and finches. There is a nice swath of trees between the palms and the lake to the north. Check this area for jays, vireos, bushtits, finches, tanagers, and a variety of migrants. A short walk north of the ruins and just west of Jacumba Street is a very brushy and weedy area. Hidden in this tangle of vegetation look for resident Bewick's Wren, Verdin, California Quail, Common Bushtit, and California Thrasher. Continue walking west up the small dike and you'll be looking over a small cattail-filled lake. Spring will find a large flock of Tricolored Blackbirds breeding there, and at other times of the year they may

107

use the marsh as a roost. The pond has been drained for extended periods in the past, but the "Trikes" favor the Jacumba area, and are usually found someplace in the vicinity. The cattails and the pond are also home to resident Pied-billed Grebe, Green Heron, and Song Sparrow. During winter and migration look for dabbling ducks, Eared Grebe, and Lincoln's Sparrow. Surprising birds visit the area on a regular basis; in the last couple of years we've seen Western Grebe, Common Loon, and Swamp Sparrow.

2) Desert Scrub

California Quail

North of the lake and the town you'll find cacti, desert brush, and some larger mesquites. In spring and summer this area is best explored in the cool of the morning hours when the birds are most vocal and active. Look for California Quail, Costa's Hummingbird, Cactus Wren, Verdin, Phainopepla, California Thrasher, and Black-throated Sparrow. In some of the rockier areas you'll find California Towhee.

3) Jacumba Hot Springs Library and Community Park

South of Old Highway 80 are a couple of buildings with large lawns and big trees, including a school, a library, and a small park. Depending on the season, glass the lawns for feeding Tricolored Blackbird, California Thrasher, and a variety of sparrows. Check the trees for American, Lesser, and Lawrence's Goldfinches.

4) Jacumba Hot Springs Neighborhoods

Drive and walk around the older portions of town to look for resident birds like California Quail, Nuttall's Woodpecker, Lesser Goldfinch, Tricolored and Brewer's Blackbirds, Western Scrub-Jay, and Western Bluebird. Breeders returning each summer include Costa's Hummingbird, Scott's and Hooded Orioles, and Lawrence's Goldfinch. Winter brings other visitors such as Northern Flicker, White-breasted Nuthatch, Mountain Chickadee, Oak Titmouse, Pine Siskin, and Cassin's Finch. Several residents feed the birds; if you find a feeding station during migration you may be treated to dozens of colorful orioles, hummingbirds, and grosbeaks all gorging themselves at one time. Check the pine tree in front of the church at Campo St. and Calexico Avenue for a resident Barn Owl. If it is still there, the whitewash on the street will give it away.

Barn Owl

5) Fields east of Jacumba Hot Springs

East of Jacumba are fields that may be fallow or under cultivation. If fallow, check them during migration and winter for Sage Thrasher, Loggerhead Shrike, White-crowned and other sparrows, and Western Meadowlark. When under cultivation check the fields for feeding Tricolored Blackbird flocks.

Driving Directions to Jacumba Hot Springs Locations

From Interstate 8 take exit 73 and head south. Turn left (southeast) onto Carrizo Gorge Road and drive 1.1 miles to Old Highway 80. Distances below are from this intersection of Carrizo Gorge Road and Old Highway 80.

- **Area 1 (Riparian Area and Cattail Pond)** – Drive west 2.0 miles to Jacumba Street. Turn right (north) and then immediately park in the gravel lot in front of the bath house ruins.

- **Area 2 (Desert Scrub)** – Drive west 2.0 miles to Jacumba Street. Turn right (north) and drive to the end of Jacumba Street. Park somewhere along the street here or along Seeley Avenue. Walk north into the desert scrub.

- **Area 3 (Jacumba Hot Springs Library and Community Park)** – Drive west 1.7 miles and park in the side lot of the library (south side of Old Highway 80). From the parking lot you can access the front of the library and also the Jacumba Community Park grounds.

- **Area 4 (Jacumba Hot Springs Neighborhoods)** – Drive west 1.6 miles to Campo Street. Turn right (north) and drive 0.1 miles to Calexico Avenue. The "Barn Owl" pine is on north side of Calexico in front of the church.

- **Area 5 (Fields East of Jacumba Hot Springs)** – Drive west on Old Highway 80 towards Jacumba, scanning the fields north of the highway for birds. Stop whenever you see an interesting bird or flock. One mile west is a dirt road that bisects the fields, allowing for closer looks at the sparrows and other birds that call this area home.

Site Notes

Best Times to Visit
- Winter has higher-elevation birds that move down out of the snow
- April has singing residents and numerous migrant passerines

Ownership
- City of Jacumba Hot Springs
- Private homes, ranches and farmland

Vehicle Access
- Good paved and gravel roads

Fees
- None

Lawrence's Goldfinch

Restrooms
- Two gas stations at I-8 at exit 73, which are 2.7 miles east and north of Jacumba

Food
- Several small restaurants and a grocery in town, all along Old Highway 80
- Subway is located in the Shell gas station at I-8, 2.7 miles out of town

Gas
- Chevron and Shell are along I-8 at exit 73, which is 2.7 miles east and north of town

S. Anza-Borrego Desert State Park Area

Habitat
- Desert washes and canyons
- Desert mountains
- Cactus forests and desert scrub
- Athel tamarisk groves
- Chaparral
- Riparian streams
- Palm groves

Target Birds
- Quail: Gambel's and California (resident)
- Golden Eagle (resident)
- Barn Owl (resident)
- Long-eared Owl (winter)
- Hummingbirds: Black-chinned (summer), Costa's (resident), Anna's (resident), and Rufous (migration)
- Sapsuckers: Red-naped and Red-breasted (winter)
- Woodpeckers: Nuttall's, Ladder-backed, and Northern Flicker (winter)
- Flycatchers: Ash-throated (summer and rarely winter)
- Loggerhead Shrike (resident)
- Verdin (resident)
- Wrens: Cactus (resident), Canyon (resident), Bewick's (resident), House (winter)
- Black-tailed Gnatcatcher (resident)
- Thrashers: Le Conte's (resident), Sage (migration and winter), California (resident), and Crissal (resident)
- Phainopepla (spring, fall, and winter)
- Black-throated Sparrow (resident)
- Bronzed Cowbird (summer)
- Orioles: Hooded (summer), Scott's (summer), and Bullock's (migration)
- Goldfinches: Lawrence's and Lesser (resident)

General Description

Anza-Borrego is the largest state park in California (1600 square miles) and offers a great diversity of habitats, from the desert valleys to pine-covered mountains. This range of habitats means a wealth of birds.

Cactus Wren

Riparian washes offer some of the highest density of avian life in the desert and feature breeding woodpeckers, hummingbirds, Phainopepla, flycatchers, Verdin, wrens, and sparrows. Migrants pause in a variety of habitats. Unique to this area are the palm oases, which feature Cactus and Rock Wrens, Scott's and Hooded Orioles, and both Great Horned and Barn Owls.

Following a wet winter, you may be treated to a wildflower spectacle. The desert floor, washes, and mountainsides all have beautiful varieties of flowers and flowering bushes.

Anza-Borrego gets its name from the Spanish explorer Juan Batista De Anza, who was one of the first Europeans to pass through the area, and "Borrego," the Spanish name for the bighorn sheep that inhabit the rugged mountain slopes towering over the desert floor. The bighorns can be anywhere on the rocky slopes, and although they can be tough to spot, it is almost guaranteed that they are watching you!

Be aware of extreme heat in the summer, when it is advisable to bird early in the morning. Flash floods, though rare, may occur during any season.

Many thanks to Bob Miller for his contributions to this chapter.

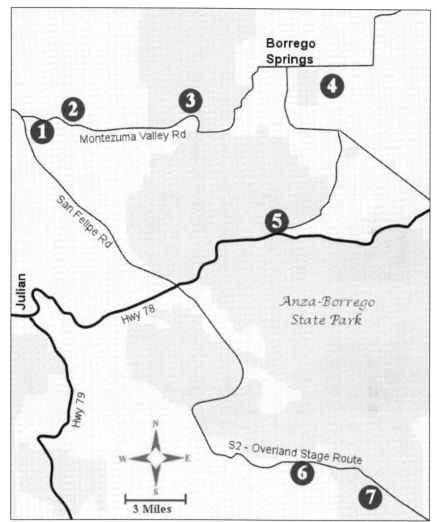

Anza Borrego State Park Area

Birding Suggestions

1) Barrel Springs

Barrel Springs, at about 3,500 feet elevation along the Pacific Crest Trail (PCT), is a short, easy walk south from the shaded parking area. There is a small concrete trough with a constant trickle of water. Sit back in the shade away from the trough and let the undisturbed parade of birds work their way down from the treetops. Goldfinches and juncos (winter) can be very numerous. Lawrence's

113

Goldfinch (winter) and Mountain Quail are often found here as well. The southbound PCT rises at a steady pace up the backside of the hill from the spring and walking a half mile or so up it can be very rewarding.

2) Old Mine Road

This unpaved, oak-tree-lined road runs a half mile through a neighborhood of a dozen or so homes and is easily birded. It attracts an unusual variety of species, some of which are more typical of higher altitudes, such as Lewis's Woodpecker (winter), Steller's Jay, and Band-tailed Pigeon. Western Scrub-Jay, Oak Titmouse, Western Bluebird, California Thrasher and Spotted Towhee are all commonly seen.

3) Big Spring

Although it is just over six miles as the crow flies, the winding S22 drops almost 4,000 ft from the divide near Ranchita to the desert floor near Borrego Springs, and the habitat types change rapidly. At the lower end of the valley, when it seems there is almost no valley left, there is a wide pullout on the north side of the road. The trail to Big Spring begins directly across from this pullout. The spring itself is several miles away, but the first quarter mile of trail across the valley floor should turn up some very good birds. A short walk north, up the small wash from the pullout, can also be very productive. California Quail, Rock and Cactus Wrens, California and Sage Thrashers, Phainopepla, Brewer's, Black-throated, White-crowned, Vesper, Savannah, and Sage Sparrows, and California Towhee are found here. Chuckwalla, a very large lizard in the iguana family, can often be seen on the large boulder piles in the summer.

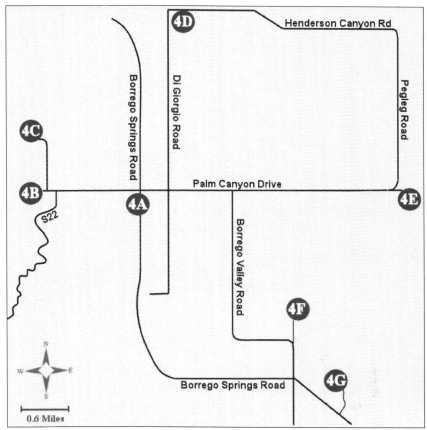

Borrego Valley

4) Borrego Valley

A - Christmas Circle

This small park in a traffic roundabout at the main intersection in the valley is the natural meeting point for most get-togethers and adventures. It has ample parking and a restroom facility. The trees attract a good number of birds, such as Western Bluebird and Anna's Hummingbird. Don't be surprised to see Greater Roadrunner.

B - Anza-Borrego Desert State Park Visitor Center

Any trip to the park should include a stop here for information on road conditions, wildflower blooms, and much more. White-winged Dove (summer), Greater Roadrunner, Costa's Hummingbird, Verdin, Cactus Wren, and Black-tailed Gnatcatcher all nest here and can be found reliably. The desert pupfish pond in front of the center and a drip on the east edge of the amphitheater provide water sources. The trees in the parking area can turn up Ladder-backed Woodpecker and the short desert scrub surrounding the parking area can have Brewer's Sparrow (migration and winter), Black-throated Sparrow and a number of others. A half-mile interpretive trail leads north toward Indianhead Peak and Borrego Palm Canyon Campground, which offers a shorter 0.25 mile trail back to the visitor center.

C - Borrego Palm Canyon Campground

Day-use parking is at the western edge of the campground at the mouth of the canyon. The entire campground is birdy. Another desert pupfish pond is a water source; desert bighorn sheep sometimes walk right up to this pond, but they are most often seen on the surrounding mountainsides. A trail leads up to the palm groves in the canyon, where Canyon Wren may be found—be prepared for a good hike if you attempt this. An alternative, very birdy trail leads out from the south end of the parking lot. Watch the hillside to the south for Rock Wren. Cactus Wren, Costa's and Anna's Hummingbirds, Black-tailed Gnatcatcher, Verdin, Brewer's and Black-throated Sparrow can be found on the desert floor. Prairie Falcon nests on the cliffs of Indianhead Peak on the north side of the canyon. Keep an eye to the sky for Golden Eagle, Swainson's (migration) and Red-tailed Hawks, and Turkey Vulture.

D - Borrego Valley Hawkwatch (BVH)

This hawkwatch is manned daily in the morning hours from the middle of February through early April. In just the few years of existence the BVH has become the premiere location for Swainson's Hawk migration in North America, with the highest spring counts. Large numbers of Turkey Vulture and small numbers of other raptors also pass through.

LeConte's Thrasher

E - Old Springs Open Space Preserve

This small dune system is home to one of the few easily accessible locations for Le Conte's Thrasher. An old borrow pit here was once the source of sand for many years of construction. The thrasher and Loggerhead Shrike are resident. "Sage" Sparrows winter here and Sage Thrasher may be found in the spring. A good way to find the Le

116

Conte's is by tracking them! Everything that happens on the sand is written there until wind and weather scour it clean (like a giant Etch A Sketch.) From the tracks of flat-tailed horned lizard, sidewinder, round-tailed ground squirrel, and red velvet mites to Common Raven and human beings, the sand records it all. A good plan is to walk southeast up the small dunes from the parking spot and make a loop east and then north around the low area of the old borrow pit. The thrashers have nested east of the borrow pit for years. Please do not play tapes at this location; patience will usually pay off.

F - Mesquite Bosque
Mesquite trees are the prominent vegetation in this low area where rainwater gathers. Crissal Thrasher, which is rare in San Diego County, is resident. Lucy's Warbler nests in the spring and Lawrence's Goldfinch may be found wintering. Walk west just over 300 ft from the pavement's end to a dirt road track. Continue north 0.5 miles to the tree line of the old Bowen Ranch property and then turn back. It is possible to drive into this area if it is dry and you have four-wheel drive.

G - Water Treatment Plant Settling Ponds
These settling ponds attract all manner of wildlife in the desert and are best birded by walking around them. Crissal Thrasher is resident in the mesquite trees on the north side of the ponds and Le Conte's Thrasher can occasionally be found here, too. Phainopepla, Black-tailed Gnatcatcher and Verdin are resident. White-crowned and Savannah Sparrows are common in the winter, and Vesper Sparrow and Lawrence's Goldfinch are sometimes found. Shorebirds like Killdeer and Least Sandpiper may also be seen here.

Black-tailed Gnatcatcher

5) Tamarisk Grove Campground and Yaqui Well
As the name implies, this is a campground with numerous athel tamarisks scattered around the campsites. A small visitor center has a list of recently spotted birds and animals. The presence of cover and water attracts a great many birds. Breeders include Bewick's Wren, Black-tailed Gnatcatcher, Ash-throated Flycatcher, Verdin, Phainopepla, Gila and Ladder-backed Woodpeckers, and both Hooded and Scott's Orioles. Winter adds to the

resident breeding population with kinglets, warblers, sometimes Lawrence's Goldfinch, and sparrows—and is a pleasant time to visit.

Migration can turn up just about any kind of bird from the mountains or the lowlands, including thrushes, warblers, vireos, tanagers, grosbeaks, and sparrows. Some years you'll find roosting Long-eared Owls, which have also nested. Barn and Great Horned Owl may also be present. Walking the entire campground loop can be quite productive. If the resident naturalist is present (winter and spring only), check to see what is being seen—including the Desert Bighorns on the mountainside to the north. Ladder-backed Woodpeckers have nest holes south of the cactus-filled roundabout by the fuel pump. There is a water drip on the corner of the fenced area at the wash's edge, south of the trees. There is also a short interpretive trail that heads up the hillside north of the campground entrance.

Yaqui Well has been a water source for centuries and is approximately 0.8 miles west of the campground. Most of the expected desert residents may be found at this desert oasis. You may supplement your list from the campground with additional quail, woodpeckers, wrens, gnatcatchers, flycatchers, California Thrasher, and other desert species. If the well is flowing during a spring visit, you may also be treated to a great variety of migrants and residents. The open top toilets are worth a visit too!

6) Vallecito Stage Station County Park

This park and Agua Caliente County Park (see next site), at about 1,500 feet, reflect the importance of water for life in the desert. Summer temperatures can be brutal and few people visit them, yet some desert residents such as California Quail, White-winged Dove, Verdin and Black-tailed Gnatcatcher will be about. Fall through spring are the best times to visit with more livable temperatures as well as a greater variety of birds. Being a bit more remote, they attract fewer visitors than the Anza-Borrego Desert State Park visitor center and Borrego Springs Valley. Earthquake fault lines here allow water to reach the surface and gather in the narrow valleys between smaller mountain ranges.

Vallecito (little valley) Stage Station is only four miles north of Agua Caliente, yet oddly averages 10 degrees cooler. It is in an open valley alongside a very dense mesquite and desert riparian area. Birding in the limited confines of the park can be very good. There are 52 campsites, eight of which are for equestrian use only. The highlight of the park is the refurbished adobe stage station; the address is "Great Southern Overland Stage Route of 1849."

7) Agua Caliente County Park

This park is nestled up against the foot of the mountains and offers several miles of excellent hiking trails. But even walking the heavily vegetated campground can turn up many of the expected desert species like Verdin, Black-tailed Gnatcatcher, Costa's Hummingbird, and Cactus Wren. There are 140 campsites and a few new rental cabins. The highlight of the park for many is swimming in the namesake hot-water mineral pools.

Ash-throated Flycatcher

Driving Directions for Anza Borrego Birding Locations

- **Area 1 (Barrel Springs)** – From the intersection of S2 (San Felipe Road) and S22 (Montezuma Valley Road) go east 1.0 miles to the parking area on the right. There is a signed walk-through gate for the Pacific Crest Trail; the spring is about 100 yards south of the gate.

- **Area 2 (Old Mine Road)** – From **Area 1** drive east 1.9 miles to Old Mine Road on the left. Go north 0.5 miles to a turnaround for passenger cars. The road continues as a designated BLM 4x4 road (Buck Canyon) past this point. It dead-ends several miles up the canyon near a small stream with nice birding and scenery. Please stay on the public road through this neighborhood.

119

- **Area 3 (Big Spring)** – From **Area 2** drive east on S22 through the community of Ranchita and over the 4,200 ft divide. At 5.9 miles will be Culp Valley Primitive Campground on the left. At 8.4 miles the Big Spring pullout will be on the left.

- **Area 4A (Borrego Valley, Christmas Circle)** – From the Big Spring pullout continue down the grade for about 6.2 miles. On the right there will be a "must see" view point of the entire Borrego Valley, and the Salton Sea on a clear day. Continue down to the stop sign on the desert floor where S22 turns right onto Palm Canyon Drive. Follow Palm Canyon Drive east for 1.4 miles to Christmas Circle in downtown Borrego Springs.

- **Area 4B (Anza-Borrego Desert State Park Visitor Center)** – From Christmas Circle go 1.8 miles west on Palm Canyon Drive and it will end in the parking lot of the visitor center.

- **Area 4C (Borrego Palm Canyon Campground)** – From **Area 4B** return east 0.2 miles and turn left on the park service road. Drive north 1.0 miles to the campground entrance station.

- **Area 4D (Borrego Valley Hawkwatch)** – From Christmas Circle go 0.5 miles east on Palm Canyon Drive to Di Giorgio Road. Turn left and drive north 4.7 miles to the hawkwatch site, which is at the end of Di Giorgio Road.

- **Area 4E (Old Springs Open Space Preserve)** – From **Area 4D** continue north 0.2 miles and turn right on Henderson Canyon Road. Drive east 4.2 miles to S22 (Pegleg Road) and turn right. (This can be one of the most popular areas in the valley if the flowers are blooming.) Drive 2.4 miles south and turn left on Old Springs Road (also called Dump Road). Drive east 0.3 miles to where the pavement turns right. Proceed past the curve for a few yards and park at the old wood fence posts. Please do not drive into the preserve.

- **Area 4F (Mesquite Bosque)** – From **Area 4E** return 0.3 miles to S22 and turn left (Pegleg Road becomes Palm Canyon Drive at this corner). Drive 2.8 miles west to Borrego Valley Road and turn left (continuing west would take you back to Christmas Circle). Drive south 3.5 miles and make a sharp turn left onto Yaqui Pass Road. Drive north on Yaqui Pass Road for 0.6 miles to the end of the pavement and park.

- **Area 4G (Water Treatment Plant Settling Ponds)** – From **Area 4F** go south 1.2 miles on Yaqui Pass Road and turn left on Borrego Springs Road. Drive east 1.1 miles and turn left onto the unnamed gravel road with three lone power poles and a rock embankment. Take the right fork and drive north 0.5 miles (there will be a rock wall on your left side) to the first corner of the two ponds. This track is solid to the halfway point, where there is a good parking area, and is usually good to the pond. However, it can be sandy on the last part, so use caution.

- **Area 5 (Tamarisk Grove Campground and Yaqui Well)** – From the intersection of Highway 78 and S3 (Yaqui Pass Road), travel northeast on Yaqui Pass Road for 0.4 miles to the entrance of Tamarisk Grove Campground. To reach Yaqui Well from the intersection of Highway 78 and Yaqui Pass Road, travel northeast on Yaqui Pass Road for 0.1 miles and turn left onto Yaqui Well Road, a sandy but generally passable road. A small sign there says "Yaqui Well Camp." Drive west on this road for 0.6 miles and park off the road in a small parking area with an information kiosk. Follow the trail north and east to Yaqui Well. There are a couple of signs, but if you miss them, just head north about 400 feet to the most vegetated spot in the wash. Be aware of possible flash flooding if there is rainy weather up canyon.

- **Area 6 (Vallecito Stage Station County Park)** – From **Area 5** at the intersection of S3 Yaqui Pass Road and Highway 78 turn right at the stop sign and go 7.0 miles to "Scissors Crossing" at S2 Great Southern Overland Stage Route and turn left. (Pacific Crest Trail, San Felipe Creek, Earthquake and Shelter Valley all come together at this crossing.) Go south 17.8 miles to the entrance on the right.

- **Area 7 (Agua Caliente County Park)** – From **Area 6** continue 3.5 miles south on S2 to Agua Caliente Spring Road. Turn right drive south 0.5 miles to the park entrance station.

Site Notes

Best Time to Visit: Spring is the best overall time with migrants passing through and residents singing, and usually the weather is ideal

Ownership
- BLM
- State of California
- Private

Vehicle Access
- Main roads and campgrounds are accessible by passenger car
- Washes, canyons, and mountain tracks are best accessed by high clearance and preferably 4x4 vehicles

Fees
- Tamarisk Grove Campground, Agua Caliente and Vallecito County Parks have day-use and camping fees

Restrooms
- Tamarisk Grove and other campgrounds
- Agua Caliente and Vallecito County Parks
- Anza-Borrego Desert State Park Headquarters
- Surrounding communities: Julian, Borrego Springs, etc.

Camping
- Borrego Palm Canyon, Tamarisk Grove and Vern Whitaker Horse Camp are the three developed campsites in Anza-Borrego State Park
- There are nine designated primitive campgrounds in Anza Borrego Desert State Park
- Anza-Borrego is the only state park that allows open primitive camping throughout the park. Check with the park for the latest rules.

Food
- Borrego Springs
- Julian

Gas
- Borrego Springs

T. Miscellaneous Birding Sites

More Birding Locations

In addition to the 19 general birding areas described in this field guide, here are 10 more very good birding locales, with a few words about each of them. And if you check the ebird site (http://ebird.org/ebird/hotspots) for San Diego hotspots, you'll find even more locations.

Fiesta Island is in Mission Bay Park, and may have fall and winter Lark Bunting, Red-throated Pipit, Chestnut-collared Longspur and, rarely, other longspurs.

Escondido Creek in Encinitas has wintering warblers and tanagers.

Hot Springs Mountain, just east of Warner Springs, is one of the last strongholds of the White-headed Woodpecker in San Diego County.

Lake Hodges, just south of Escondido, has breeding Bald Eagle and many wintering waterfowl.

Liberty Station is close to the airport and has a good array of migrant kingbirds and warblers.

Otay Lakes have gulls, California Gnatcatcher, and wintering Bell's Sparrow. The lakes are located in extreme southern San Diego County east of Chula Vista.

Ramona Grasslands Preserve is known for its winter collection of Bald and Golden Eagles, Ferruginous Hawk, and both Western and Mountain Bluebirds. It is 6.2 miles west of central Ramona.

Rohr Park, east of Chula Vista, often has wintering Baltimore Oriole.

San Diego Zoo has a wide variety of migrants and vagrants; it is situated in Balboa Park (see Chapter A).

Sweetwater Reservoir, east of Chula Vista, has wintering Bald Eagle and waterfowl.

Offshore Pelagic Trips can yield a fine variety of boobies, shearwaters, alcids, scoters, tropicbirds, phalaropes, gulls, and terns. Each season offers varied and exciting opportunities. Look for a schedule at http://www.socalbirding.com/.

U. San Diego County Bird Checklist

Seasons

Spring is Mar-May
Summer is Jun-Aug
Fall is Sep-Nov
Winter is Dec-Feb

Status Codes

These "Status Codes" are the likelihood of finding a particular bird species if you look for it in the right type of habitat, at the right time of year, and at the right time of day.

C - Common, usually seen 3 out of 4 visits
U - Uncommon, may be seen 1 out of 4 visits
R - Rare, usually not seen, and may be absent some years
V - Vagrant, not expected in this area on a regular basis—may be a
visitor from Mexico, Asia, or the eastern United States

Notes

B - Confirmed or probable breeding
I - Irregular, may be present some years and absent others

This checklist is in A.O.U. (7th Edition) order, 56th supplement, from July 2015.

This list of 406 birds contains the vast majority of species that have been observed in San Diego County over the past fifteen years. Vagrants or accidentals which have only been spotted once or twice are not included. However, just about any migratory bird that breeds in the United States has the potential to show up here, so make sure to bring along a comprehensive bird guide.

A complete list of 660 birds found in California and accepted by the California Bird Records Committee is at: http://www.californiabirds.org.

	Notes	Spr	Sum	Fall	Win
Anatidae - Swans, Geese, Ducks					
Greater White-fronted Goose		U	R	U	U
Snow Goose		U	R	U	U
Ross's Goose		U	R	U	U
Brant		C	R	C	C
Cackling Goose		R	R	R	R
Canada Goose	B	C	C	C	C
Tundra Swan					R
Wood Duck		C	C	C	C
Gadwall	B	C	C	C	C
Eurasian Wigeon		V		V	V
American Wigeon		C	R	C	C
Mallard	B	C	C	C	C
Blue-winged Teal		C	R	C	C
Cinnamon Teal	B	U	U	C	C
Northern Shoveler	B	C	U	C	C
Northern Pintail	B	C	R	C	C
Green-winged Teal	B	C	R	C	C
Canvasback		U	R	U	U
Redhead	B	C	U	C	C
Ring-necked Duck		C	R	C	C
Tufted Duck		V			V
Greater Scaup		R		U	C
Lesser Scaup		U	R	C	C
Harlequin Duck		V			V
Surf Scoter		C	R	C	C
White-winged Scoter		R		R	R
Black Scoter		R		R	R
Long-tailed Duck		R		R	R
Bufflehead		C	R	C	C
Common Goldeneye		U		U	C
Hooded Merganser		R		U	U
Common Merganser		R		U	U
Red-breasted Merganser		U	R	U	C
Ruddy Duck	B	C	C	C	C

Odontophoridae - Quail					
Mountain Quail	B	U	U	U	U
California Quail	B	C	C	C	C
Gambel's Quail	B	U	U	U	U
Phasianidae - Partridges, Grouse, and Turkey					
Wild Turkey	B	C	C	C	C
Gaviidae - Loons					
Red-throated Loon		U		U	C
Pacific Loon		C	R	C	C
Common Loon		C	R	C	C
Yellow-billed Loon		V		V	V
Podicipedidae - Grebes					
Pied-billed Grebe	B	C	C	C	C
Horned Grebe		U		U	C
Red-necked Grebe					V
Eared Grebe	B	C	U	C	C
Western Grebe	B	C	C	C	C
Clark's Grebe	B	C	C	C	C
Procellariidae - Shearwaters					
Northern Fulmar		R		R	R
Pink-footed Shearwater		R		R	U
Flesh-footed Shearwater		R	R	R	
Sooty Shearwater		U	U	R	
Short-tailed Shearwater				R	U
Black-vented Shearwater				U	U
Hydrobatidae - Storm-Petrels					
Ashy Storm-Petrel				R	R
Black Storm-Petrel			U	U	
Phaethontidae - Tropicbirds					
Red-billed Tropicbird			R	R	
Fregatidae - Frigatebirds					
Magnificent Frigatebird		R	U	U	R
Sulidae - Boobies					
Masked Booby			V	V	V
Brown Booby			U	U	R
Phalacrocoracidae - Cormorants					
Brandt's Cormorant	B	C	C	C	C
Double-crested Cormorant	B	C	C	C	C

126

Pelagic Cormorant		U	R	U	U
Pelecanidae - Pelicans					
American White Pelican		C	U	C	C
Brown Pelican		C	C	C	C
Ardeidae - Herons, Bitterns, and Allies					
American Bittern	B	U	U	U	U
Least Bittern	B	U	U	U	U
Great Blue Heron	B	C	C	C	C
Great Egret	B	C	C	C	C
Snowy Egret	B	C	C	C	C
Little Blue Heron	B	C	C	C	C
Tricolored Heron				V	V
Reddish Egret		R	R	C	U
Cattle Egret	B	U	U	U	U
Green Heron	B	C	C	C	C
Black-crowned Night-Heron	B	C	C	C	C
Yellow-crowned Night-Heron	B	U	U	U	U
Threskiornithidae - Ibises, Spoonbills					
White-faced Ibis	B	U	U	U	C
Cathartidae - New World Vultures					
Black Vulture		V	V	V	V
Turkey Vulture	B	C	C	C	C
Pandionidae - Osprey					
Osprey	B	C	C	C	C
Accipitridae - Kites, Eagles, Hawks					
White-tailed Kite	B	C	C	C	C
Bald Eagle	B	U	U	U	C
Northern Harrier	B	U	U	C	C
Sharp-shinned Hawk		U		U	U
Cooper's Hawk	B	C	C	C	C
Harris's Hawk		R	R	R	R
Red-shouldered Hawk	B	C	C	C	C
Swainson's Hawk		U		U	
Zone-tailed Hawk	B	R		R	R
Red-tailed Hawk	B	C	C	C	C
Rough-legged Hawk				R	R
Ferruginous Hawk		R		U	U
Golden Eagle	B	R	R	R	R

Rallidae - Rails, Gallinules, Coots					
Black Rail					V
Ridgway's Rail	B	C	C	C	C
Virginia Rail	B	C	C	C	C
Sora		C	R	C	C
Common Gallinule	B	C	C	C	C
American Coot	B	C	C	C	C
Gruidae - Cranes					
Sandhill Crane				R	R
Recurvirostridae - Stilts, Avocets					
Black-necked Stilt	B	C	C	C	C
American Avocet	B	C	C	C	C
Haematopodidae - Oystercatchers					
American Oystercatcher		R		R	R
Black Oystercatcher		R	R	U	U
Charadriidae - Plovers					
Black-bellied Plover		C	U	C	C
American Golden-Plover		R		R	
Pacific Golden-Plover		R		R	R
Snowy Plover	B	C	C	C	C
Wilson's Plover		V	V	V	
Semipalmated Plover		U	U	C	C
Killdeer	B	C	C	C	C
Mountain Plover				R	R
Scolopacidae - Sandpipers, Phalaropes					
Spotted Sandpiper		U	R	C	U
Solitary Sandpiper		R		U	R
Wandering Tattler		U		U	U
Greater Yellowlegs		C	U	C	C
Willet		C	C	C	C
Lesser Yellowlegs		U	U	C	U
Upland Sandpiper				V	
Whimbrel		U	U	C	U
Long-billed Curlew		C	U	C	C
Bar-tailed Godwit				V	V
Marbled Godwit		C	U	C	C
Ruddy Turnstone		C	R	C	C
Black Turnstone		C	R	C	C

Red Knot	C	U	C	U
Surfbird	C		U	U
Ruff			V	V
Stilt Sandpiper			R	
Sanderling	C	U	C	C
Dunlin	U		U	U
Baird's Sandpiper			U	
Least Sandpiper	C	U	C	C
Buff-breasted Sandpiper			R	
Pectoral Sandpiper			R	
Semipalmated Sandpiper	V			
Western Sandpiper	U		U	
Short-billed Dowitcher	C		C	C
Long-billed Dowitcher	C	R	C	C
Wilson's Snipe	U		U	U
Wilson's Phalarope	U		U	
Red-necked Phalarope	U		U	
Red Phalarope	R		R	R
Stercorariidae - Skuas				
South Polar Skua	R		R	
Pomarine Jaeger	U	R	U	R
Parasitic Jaeger	R		U	R
Long-tailed Jaeger			R	
Alcidae – Auks, Murres, and Puffins				
Common Murre	U		R	U
Craveri's Murrelet		R	R	
Ancient Murrelet			R	R
Cassin's Auklet			R	R
Rhinoceros Auklet			R	U
Laridae - Gulls, Terns				
Black-legged Kittiwake			R	R
Sabine's Gull	R		U	
Bonaparte's Gull	U	R	U	C
Laughing Gull	V	V	V	V
Franklin's Gull	R		U	
Heermann's Gull	U	U	C	C
Mew Gull			R	U
Ring-billed Gull	C	U	C	C

Western Gull	B	C	C	C	C
California Gull		C	R	C	C
Herring Gull		U		U	U
Thayer's Gull				R	R
Lesser Black-backed Gull		R		R	R
Glaucous-winged Gull		R		R	U
Glaucous Gull					R
Least Tern	B	U	C	C	
Gull-billed Tern	B	U	U	U	
Caspian Tern	B	C	C	U	R
Black Tern		U	R	U	
Common Tern			R	U	
Forster's Tern	B	C	C	C	U
Royal Tern	B	U	R	C	C
Elegant Tern	B	U	C	C	R
Black Skimmer	B	U	C	U	U
Columbidae - Pigeons, Doves					
Rock Pigeon	B	C	C	C	C
Eurasian Collared-Dove	B	C	C	C	C
Inca Dove	B	U	U	U	U
Common Ground-Dove	B	U	U	U	U
White-winged Dove	B	C	C	U	R
Mourning Dove	B	C	C	C	C
Cuculidae - Cuckoos, Roadrunners					
Yellow-billed Cuckoo			R		
Greater Roadrunner	B	U	U	U	U
Tytonidae - Barn Owls					
Barn Owl	B	U	U	U	U
Strigidae - Typical Owls					
Flammulated Owl		R	R		
Western Screech-Owl	B	U	U	U	U
Great Horned Owl	B	C	C	C	C
Burrowing Owl	B	U	U	U	U
Spotted Owl	B	U	U	U	U
Long-eared Owl	B	R	R	R	R
Short-eared Owl		R		R	R
Northern Saw-whet Owl	B	U	U	U	U

Caprimulgidae - Nighthawks, Nightjars					
Lesser Nighthawk	B	U	C	C	R
Common Poorwill		U	U		
Apodidae - Swifts					
Black Swift		R	R		
Chimney Swift		R	R		
Vaux's Swift		C		U	
White-throated Swift	B	U	U	U	U
Trochilidae - Hummingbirds					
Black-chinned Hummingbird	B	C	C	U	
Anna's Hummingbird	B	C	C	C	C
Costa's Hummingbird	B	C	U	U	U
Calliope Hummingbird		R	R	R	
Rufous Hummingbird		U	U	C	
Allen's Hummingbird	B	U	U	C	U
Alcedinidae - Kingfishers					
Belted Kingfisher	B	U	R	U	C
Picidae - Woodpeckers					
Lewis's Woodpecker		R		R	R
Acorn Woodpecker	B	C	C	C	C
Williamson's Sapsucker					R
Yellow-bellied Sapsucker					V
Red-naped Sapsucker		R		R	R
Red-breasted Sapsucker		R	U	R	R
Ladder-backed Woodpecker	B	U	U	U	U
Nuttall's Woodpecker	B	C	C	C	C
Downy Woodpecker	B	U	U	U	U
Hairy Woodpecker	B	U	U	U	U
White-headed Woodpecker	B	R	R	R	R
Northern Flicker	B	C	C	C	C
Falconidae - Caracaras, Falcons					
Crested Caracara		V	V	V	V
American Kestrel	B	C	C	C	C
Merlin		R		R	U
Peregrine Falcon	B	U	U	U	U
Prairie Falcon	B	R	R	R	U
Psittacidae – African and New World Parrots					
Red-crowned Parrot	B	U	U	U	U

Tyrannidae - Tyrant Flycatchers					
Olive-sided Flycatcher	B	U	U	U	
Western Wood-Pewee	B	C	C	C	
Willow Flycatcher	B	U	U	U	
Hammond's Flycatcher		U		R	
Gray Flycatcher		R		R	R
Dusky Flycatcher	B	U	U	U	
Pacific-slope Flycatcher	B	C	C	C	R
Black Phoebe	B	C	C	C	C
Eastern Phoebe		V		V	V
Say's Phoebe	B	C	C	C	C
Vermilion Flycatcher	B	C	U	U	C
Ash-throated Flycatcher	B	C	C	C	R
Brown-crested Flycatcher	B	U	U	U	
Tropical Kingbird				V	V
Cassin's Kingbird	B	C	C	C	C
Thick-billed Kingbird		V			V
Western Kingbird	B	C	C	C	
Scissor-tailed Flycatcher		V	V	V	V
Laniidae - Shrikes					
Loggerhead Shrike	B	U	U	U	C
Vireonidae - Vireos					
Bell's Vireo	B	C	C	U	
Gray Vireo	B	U	U	U	
Plumbeous Vireo		R		R	R
Cassin's Vireo	B	R	R	R	R
Hutton's Vireo	B	C	C	C	C
Warbling Vireo	B	C	R	C	
Red-eyed Vireo		V		V	
Yellow-green Vireo				V	
Corvidae – Crows and Jays					
Pinyon Jay	I	V		V	V
Clark's Nutcracker	I	V		V	V
Steller's Jay	B	C	C	C	C
Western Scrub-Jay	B	C	C	C	C
American Crow	B	C	C	C	C
Common Raven	B	C	C	C	C
Alaudidae - Larks					

Horned Lark	B	U	U	C	C
Hirundinidae - Swallows					
Purple Martin	B	R	R	R	
Tree Swallow	B	C	R	C	C
Violet-green Swallow	B	C	C	C	
Northern Rough-winged Swallow	B	C	C	C	R
Bank Swallow		R		R	
Cliff Swallow	B	C	C	C	
Barn Swallow	B	C	U	U	U
Paridae - Chickadees and Titmice					
Mountain Chickadee	B	C	C	C	C
Oak Titmouse	B	C	C	C	C
Remizidae - Verdins					
Verdin	B	C	C	C	C
Aegithalidae - Bushtits					
Bushtit	B	C	C	C	C
Sittidae - Nuthatches					
Red-breasted Nuthatch	B	R	R	R	R
White-breasted Nuthatch	B	C	C	C	C
Certhiidae - Creepers					
Brown Creeper	B	U	U	U	U
Troglodytidae - Wrens					
Rock Wren	B	C	C	C	C
Canyon Wren	B	U	U	U	U
House Wren	B	C	C	C	C
Pacific Wren		R		R	R
Marsh Wren	B	C	C	C	C
Bewick's Wren	B	C	C	C	C
Cactus Wren	B	C	C	C	C
Sylviidae - Gnatcatchers					
Blue-gray Gnatcatcher	B	C	C	C	C
California Gnatcatcher	B	C	C	U	U
Black-tailed Gnatcatcher	B	C	C	C	C
Cinclidae - Dippers					
American Dipper	B	R	R	R	R
Regulidae - Kinglets					
Golden-crowned Kinglet	B	R	R	R	R
Ruby-crowned Kinglet		C		C	C

133

Sylviidae - Sylviid Warblers					
Wrentit	B	C	C	C	C
Turdidae - Thrushes					
Western Bluebird	B	C	C	C	C
Mountain Bluebird	I	R		U	U
Townsend's Solitaire		R		R	R
Swainson's Thrush	B	C	R	R	
Hermit Thrush	B	U	U	U	C
American Robin	B	C	C	C	C
Varied Thrush	I	R		R	R
Mimidae – Mockingbirds and Thrashers					
Gray Catbird		V			V
Brown Thrasher		V		V	V
California Thrasher	B	C	C	C	C
Le Conte's Thrasher	B	R	R	R	R
Crissal Thrasher	B	U	U	U	U
Sage Thrasher		U		R	R
Northern Mockingbird	B	C	C	C	C
Sturnidae - Starlings					
European Starling	B	C	C	C	C
Motacillidae - Pipits					
Red-throated Pipit				V	V
American Pipit		U		U	C
Sprague's Pipit					R
Bombycillidae - Waxwings					
Cedar Waxwing	I	C		C	C
Ptilogonatidae - Silky-flycatchers					
Phainopepla	B	C	U	C	C
Calcariidae - Longspurs					
Lapland Longspur				R	R
Chestnut-collared Longspur				R	R
McCown's Longspur				R	R
Parulidae - Wood Warblers					
Ovenbird				V	V
Worm-eating Warbler				V	
Northern Waterthrush				V	
Black-and-white Warbler		R		R	R
Tennessee Warbler				V	

Orange-crowned Warbler	B	C	C	C	C
Lucy's Warbler	B	R	R	R	
Nashville Warbler		C		U	R
Virginia's Warbler		V		V	V
MacGillivray's Warbler		C		U	
Common Yellowthroat	B	C	C	C	C
Hooded Warbler		V		V	V
American Redstart		V		V	V
Cape May Warbler		V		V	
Northern Parula		R	R	R	R
Magnolia Warbler		V	V	V	V
Bay-breasted Warbler		V		V	
Yellow Warbler	B	C	U	U	R
Chestnut-sided Warbler		V		V	V
Blackpoll Warbler		V		V	
Black-throated Blue Warbler		V		V	V
Palm Warbler		V		V	V
Pine Warbler		V		V	V
Yellow-rumped Warbler	B	C	U	C	C
Yellow-throated Warbler		V		V	V
Prairie Warbler				V	V
Grace's Warbler		V		V	V
Black-throated Gray Warbler	B	C	U	C	R
Townsend's Warbler		U		U	U
Hermit Warbler		U		R	R
Black-throated Green Warbler		V		V	V
Canada Warbler		V		V	
Wilson's Warbler	B	C	R	C	R
Painted Redstart		V		V	V
Yellow-breasted Chat	B	C	C	U	
Emberizidae - Emberizine Finches					
Green-tailed Towhee	B	R	R	R	R
Spotted Towhee	B	C	C	C	C
Rufous-crowned Sparrow	B	U	U	U	U
California Towhee	B	C	C	C	C
Abert's Towhee	B	C	C	C	C
Chipping Sparrow	B	C	U	U	U
Clay-colored Sparrow		R			R

Brewer's Sparrow	B	C	R	C	C
Black-chinned Sparrow	B	U	U	R	R
Vesper Sparrow		C		C	C
Lark Sparrow	B	C	U	C	C
Black-throated Sparrow	B	C	C	C	C
Sagebrush Sparrow					U
Bell's Sparrow	B	U	U	U	U
Savannah Sparrow	B	C	U	C	C
Grasshopper Sparrow	B	U	U	R	R
Nelson's Sparrow				V	V
Fox Sparrow	B	U	U	U	C
Song Sparrow	B	C	C	C	C
Lincoln's Sparrow		U		C	C
Swamp Sparrow				R	R
White-throated Sparrow		V		V	V
Harris's Sparrow		V		V	V
White-crowned Sparrow		C		C	C
Golden-crowned Sparrow		U		U	C
Dark-eyed Junco	B	C	C	C	C
Cardinalidae – Cardinals and Allies					
Hepatic Tanager				V	V
Summer Tanager	B	R	R	R	R
Scarlet Tanager		V		V	
Western Tanager	B	C	U	C	R
Rose-breasted Grosbeak		V	V	V	V
Black-headed Grosbeak	B	C	C	C	R
Blue Grosbeak	B	C	C	U	R
Lazuli Bunting	B	C	C	C	
Indigo Bunting	B	R	R	V	
Painted Bunting				V	
Icteridae - Blackbirds					
Bobolink				V	
Red-winged Blackbird	B	C	C	C	C
Tricolored Blackbird	B	U	C	C	U
Western Meadowlark	B	C	C	C	C
Yellow-headed Blackbird	B	U	U	U	U
Brewer's Blackbird	B	C	C	C	C
Great-tailed Grackle	B	C	C	C	C

Bronzed Cowbird	B	U	U		
Brown-headed Cowbird	B	C	C	C	C
Orchard Oriole		V		V	V
Hooded Oriole	B	C	C	U	R
Baltimore Oriole		V		V	V
Bullock's Oriole	B	C	U	U	V
Scott's Oriole	B	C	C	U	R
Fringillidae – Finches and Allies					
House Finch	B	C	C	C	C
Purple Finch	B	C	C	C	C
Cassin's Finch	I	R		R	R
Red Crossbill	I	R		R	R
Pine Siskin		R		R	U
Lesser Goldfinch	B	C	C	C	C
Lawrence's Goldfinch	B	U	C	U	U
American Goldfinch	B	U	U	U	U
Evening Grosbeak	I				V
Passeridae - Old World Sparrows					
House Sparrow	B	C	C	C	C
Estrildidae - Waxbills and Allies					
Scaly-breasted Munia	B	C	C	C	C

137

INDEX

139

142

44443021R00091

Made in the USA
San Bernardino, CA
15 January 2017